The Changing Distribution of the Social Wage

Tom Sefton

ISBN 0 7530 0106 3

Suntory and Toyota International Centres for Economics and Related Disciplines
London School of Economics and Political Science
Houghton Street
London WC2A 2AE, UK

Printed in Great Britain by
Print Fast
20 Rathbone Place
London W1P 1DG, UK

Contents
Page

i

Acknowledgements

This report is based on research funded by the Joseph Rowntree Foundation to whom the author is very grateful. All opinions are, however, those of the author, not necessarily of the Foundation, nor of the Department of the Environment, from which the author was on leave of absence to the LSE Welfare State Programme as a Research Officer at the time of writing.

The author would particularly like to thank John Hills for his continuous support and guidance throughout the project and Maria Evandrou and Jane Falkingham, who helped to direct the research, for their expert advice. The author is also grateful for the valuable contribution of the Advisory Group, which included Gordon Harris, Stephen Jenkins, Julian Le Grand, Nigel Stuttard, Steven Webb and Derek Williams, and to Stephen Aldridge for his comments on the final draft. Thanks are due to Jane Dickson, who did a tireless job in preparing the script, and to Brian Warren, Nick Warner and John Wild for providing IT support.

Data from the Family Expenditure Survey, the General Household Survey, and Building Societies Mortgages 5% sample, and Households Below Average Incomes were kindly made available through the ESRC Data Archive at Essex University. Officials at various Government Departments were also very helpful in responding to endless questions and requests for data. Interpretation of these data is the author's responsibility.

ii

Executive Summary

Introduction

A third of all public spending in the United Kingdom is on welfare services such as the National Health Service, state education, personal social services, and subsidised social housing. The distribution of this "social wage" is important in distributional terms because apportioning the value of these services to those who benefit from them is likely to have a significant equalising effect.

The report builds on previous research by:

- allowing for variations in the use of services that are related to socio-economic characteristics and to incomes;

- taking into account expenditure on the non-household population, including people in residential homes and students living in halls of residence;

- using an economic approach, rather than an accounting one to put a value on benefits in kind;

- examining changes in the distribution of the social wage on a consistent basis over the period since 1979 and seeking to account for these changes;

- exploring local variations in spending on welfare services.

The overall distribution of the social wage

Our estimates of the distribution of benefits in kind show that:

- The distribution of the social wage is fairly 'pro-poor' in that lower income groups receive a greater absolute value of benefits in kind from welfare services than do higher income groups. In 1993, the value of benefits in kind received by the bottom quintile group (i.e. the poorest fifth of the population) was about 70 per cent greater than for the top quintile group.

- The degree of this pro-poor bias varies significantly between services. Housing and personal social services are both strongly pro-poor. Schools (including further education) and health care are moderately pro-poor, while higher education is strongly pro-rich (see Table 1).

- The degree to which the distribution is pro-poor cannot be accounted for by demographic factors alone. Controlling for

1

differences in service use related to age and gender, the distribution of the social wage is still pro-poor, though the bias in favour of the poor is considerably reduced.

Table 1: The Distribution of Benefits in Kind, 1993

Service	Ratio of spending per person on the bottom quintile group to that on the top quintile group	
	Actual	Demographically-adjusted
Subsidised social housing	9.9	6.2
Personal social services	7.9	1.1
Schools and further education	2.2	1.1
Health care	1.3	1.1
Higher education	0.5	0.7
All services	1.7	1.2

Distributional changes since 1979

Between 1979-93, the overall value of the social wage increased by around 30 per cent in real terms:

- Lower income groups benefited more from the increase in the social wage than higher income groups. Thus, the distribution has become more pro-poor over the period.

- Demographic changes *reduced* the overall pressure on welfare services. This was because the effects of a falling child population on education spending more than offset the effects of an ageing population on health care and personal social services spending. The reduction in demographic pressures was greatest for higher income groups, which is the main reason they experienced a smaller increase in benefits in kind.

- Other non-demographic factors, including changes in government policy, also favoured lower income groups, although only marginally. The proportion of benefits in kind received by the poorest 50 per cent of the population increased by four percentage points between 1979-93. But, once demographic changes are adjusted for, the share received by the poorest 50 per cent increased by less than one percentage point (see Table 2).

Table 2: Changes in Distribution of the Social Wage, 1979-93

	Change in the share of benefits in kind received by the poorest 50 per cent of the population:	
	Actual (%)	Demographically-adjusted(%)
1979	56.0	52.9
1993	60.1	53.7
Change: 1979-93	+4.1	+0.8

Impact on income inequality

Adding the value of benefits in kind to cash incomes has an equalising effect on incomes. Changes in the social wage have also affected trends in inequality over time:

- Changes in the social wage have not prevented inequality from rising, but they have helped to offset the increased inequality of cash incomes. According to a standard measure of inequality, the Gini coefficient, the increase in inequality since 1979 is smaller by around one fifth, once the social wage effect is taken into account (see Table 3).

- While the cash incomes of the bottom quintile group grew only slightly over the period (by around 6 per cent), final incomes (which include the social wage) grew by between 6-13 per cent, depending on how cost inflation is adjusted for.

Table 3: Measures of Income Inequality, 1979-93

Gini coefficients	1979	1987	1993	Change: 1979-93
Cash incomes	0.241	0.305	0.334	0.093
Final incomes	0.212	0.260	0.286	0.074
Social wage effect	-0.029	-0.045	-0.048	-0.019

Service-by-service analysis

Health care

- All income groups benefited from real increases in NHS expenditure between 1979-93, but middle income groups benefited more than the bottom income group. In 1979, lower income groups made the greatest use of health care services, after standardising for differences related to age and gender. By 1993,

3

demographically-adjusted spending on health care was greater for people in the second and third quintile groups;

- Other policy changes cancelled each other out over the period. A reduction in spending on elderly people relative to other age groups favoured higher income groups, while increases in charges favoured lower income groups. Changes in the regional allocation of NHS resources had only a slight (pro-poor) effect on the distribution between income groups.

Schools and further education

- Demographic factors are largely responsible for the shape of the distribution and the way it has changed since 1979. However, there is an underlying bias in favour of lower income groups, because they make less use of private schools;

- The impact of non-demographic factors was fairly neutral over the period. Higher income groups experienced the biggest increases in participation rates for pupils aged under 18. But lower income groups benefited from an increase in spending per pupil on schools relative to further education.

Higher education

- The bottom income group benefited more than other income groups from the increase in higher education spending , but the distribution is still heavily skewed in favour of higher income groups. If demographic effects are controlled for, the increase in spending was greatest for the top income group (in both absolute and proportional terms);

- Higher income groups have benefited most from the expansion in the number of *non-mature* students, but were hardest hit by the reduction in funding per student and by cuts in maintenance payments.

Housing

- The overall value of housing benefits in kind has remained almost unchanged over the period, but the distribution has shifted in favour of lower income groups. While the proportion of council tenants has fallen, especially in higher income groups, the average subsidy per council property in economic terms has risen.

- Right To Buy subsidies are less pro-poor in their distribution than subsidies to council tenants. However, the net impact of the scheme is a reduction in the value of benefits in kind, because households would probably have received a larger economic subsidy if they had remained as tenants (at current rents, etc).

Personal Social Services

- The distribution of spending on personal social services for the elderly is strongly pro-poor, but much of this is accounted for by the fact that there are more elderly people in the bottom half of the income distribution.
- The pro-poor bias of the distribution (after adjusting for demographic factors) is stronger within the retired population than within the population as a whole. But, even within the retired population, it is not the poorest who are benefiting the most.

Chapter One: Introduction

Background

A third of all public spending in the United Kingdom is on welfare services 'in kind' such as the National Health Service, state education, personal social services, and subsidised social housing. In recent years, this "social wage" has constituted around one eighth of Gross Domestic Product. Its size is therefore significant in relation to cash incomes. In distributional terms this is important, because apportioning the value of these services to those who benefit from them is likely to have a significant equalising effect. The social wage, taken as a whole, is fairly evenly distributed across income groups, while net cash incomes are distributed unequally. It is therefore worth proportionally more to lower income groups than to higher income groups.

The value of government spending on these services has also increased substantially since 1979 in real (RPI-adjusted) terms, although their total has increased only slightly in relation to GDP (see Figure 1.1). Depending on how the distribution between income groups has changed over time, it is possible that changes in the social wage have partly offset the growing inequality of cash incomes. Indeed, one criticism of the 1995 Joseph Rowntree Report on *Income and Wealth* was that it ignored the value of the social wage (Cooper and Nye, 1995). One of the questions addressed in this report is whether allowing for benefits in kind alters the view that the poorest groups in society have failed to benefit from recent economic growth. In other words, is it the case that the poor have benefited from economic growth through higher spending on health care, education, and other public services, even if the amount they receive in cash incomes has not increased in line with average incomes?

Variations in people's use of welfare services are of interest in themselves. Recent research has challenged earlier suggestions that, far from benefiting the poorest, welfare services had been "captured" by the middle classes (Le Grand, 1982). However, the question as to who is benefiting most from the welfare state is still a controversial issue. This report does not address in detail the relationship between needs and provision, but it does provide a more complete picture than before as to how welfare spending varies with people's income, age, gender, tenure, region, and other relevant characteristics.

A better understanding of how welfare spending is allocated between people is also important in assessing the distributional impact

Figure 1.1: Public Expenditure on Welfare Services, 1979-93

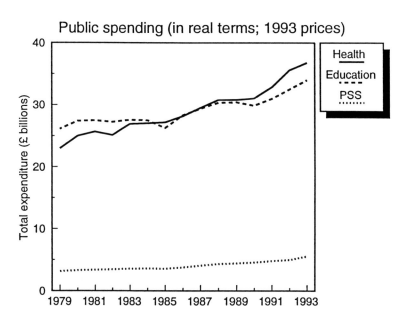

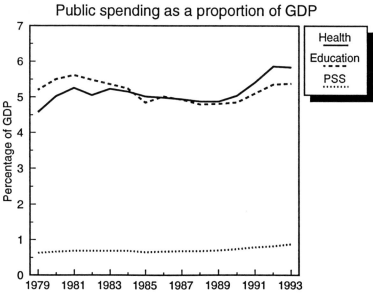

of government policies. For example, to evaluate a policy which involves a change in taxation accompanied by an increase or reduction in public services, it is necessary to take into account the distributional effects of the latter, as well as the former. (Only the effects of changes in taxation would be captured by looking at cash incomes.) This is very relevant at a time when there is strong pressure to contain government spending on public services. Those people who are making most use of public services stand to lose most if spending on these services is cut back or, more radically, there is a shift away from public provision towards private insurance.

Conceptual issues

Objectives of welfare services

Interest in the distribution of the social wage depends on the significance attached to the redistributive role of welfare services. For some, the primary aim of providing free or subsidised public services is to redistribute between rich and poor. Whether welfare services are successful can therefore be judged by looking at how much people in different income groups are making use of these services. Of course, there is also a need to justify the provision of 'in kind' benefits as opposed to cash transfers (which people could spend on services as they pleased). One argument is that redistribution is more politically acceptable if the net 'donors' can be sure how the money is being spent. A more paternalistic version of this argument is that the recipients do not necessarily know what is good for them, and so certain services should be subsidised to encourage their use or made compulsory.

The most fundamental critique of this approach is that the welfare state was never designed as an instrument for redistributing from rich to poor, so it is largely irrelevant whether this 'non-objective' is being achieved. Proponents of this view would argue that what matters is not how much people are actually using a service, but the principle that everyone is entitled to use that service without discrimination, including on the basis of ability to pay (Powell, 1995). Universal services generate a kind of 'social citizenship'. They point out that if the aim were to redistribute to the poor, then selective targeted services - not universal services - would have been more effective.

An intermediate view is that redistribution is an important objective of the welfare services, but it is not the only objective. For example, much of what the welfare state does is to provide social insurance against adverse situations, such as unemployment or ill-health. Redistribution takes place not between rich and poor, but between the employed and unemployed or between healthy and sick people, which may be the same people at different points in their life. State provision of particular services can also be justified on efficiency grounds, where the market might fail to deliver a desirable outcome. In the case of health care, for example, the consumer may not have sufficient information about what they are buying to enable a private market to operate effectively. The greater the importance attached to other objectives, the less significance will be attached to the redistributional objective.

A more subtle distinction is between the objective of redistributing from rich to poor and the objective of equality. Many analyses of the distribution of welfare services do not test whether they are redistributing from rich to poor per se, but whether they are achieving some notion of equality. The relationship between the two depends very much on how equality is defined. If equality is defined broadly in terms of achieving a greater *equality of final incomes* (i.e. cash incomes plus social wage), then services that are concentrated on poorer people will also contribute towards greater equality. On the other hand, equality is often defined more specifically for individual services in terms of achieving *equal provision for equal need*. In this case, redistributing from rich to poor will only be consistent with the equality objective if it can also be shown that poorer people have greater needs. Similarly, equality of *outcome* is only consistent with redistribution from rich to poor if it can be shown that poorer people require more health care to achieve the same level of health or more education to achieve the same academic results.

Pro-rich or pro-poor?

If we accept that the distribution of benefits between rich and poor is an important issue, there is still a need to define more precisely how the distributional bias of services is to be assessed. The simplest way is to compare the value of benefits received by different income groups. This is the basic criteria used throughout this report. Services are described as pro-poor if more is spent on lower income groups than on higher income groups.

However, this ignores differences in need. In the area of health care, the debate has centred not on whether poorer people are receiving less than richer people, but whether they are receiving less than rich people in relation to their medical needs. If poor people are using more of a service, but they also have greater needs, is it still reasonable to describe the distribution as pro-poor? For this reason, many of our results are standardised for differences in the use of services that are related to age and gender, both of which are key determinants of the need for welfare services. But other non-demographic factors affect need, too. For example, surveys of self-reported morbidity suggest that, other things being equal, poorer people have higher rates of morbidity (or ill-health) than richer people (O'Donnell and Propper, 1991). Thus, on the basis of need, we might expect some pro-poor bias even in the demographically-adjusted distribution of welfare services.

Another issue concerns the time period over which distributional questions are analysed. In this report, the analysis is based on a 'snapshot' of the population in a particular year. Thus, the health care system will appear to be redistributing in favour of elderly people in the population. But, with a longer time horizon, most of the redistribution would be taking place across people's own life cycles rather than between different people. Thus, extending the period of analysis would reduce the extent of any distribution between rich and poor (Falkingham and Hills, 1995).

A final consideration not addressed in this report is the distributional effects of taxes needed to finance public expenditure on welfare services. Even if the distribution of public spending were uniform across income groups, the net effect (including the effects of taxation) would still be redistributive, because a greater proportion of tax revenue is paid by higher income groups. In fact, to be strictly neutral, the distribution of benefits in kind would have to be as pro-rich as the tax payments used to finance them. Thus, to say that the distribution of a particular service is pro-rich (in the sense used in this report) does not mean that lower income groups would be better off if the service were scrapped altogether. The answer to this would depend on how the money saved were used. If it were used to finance lower income taxes, for example, then it is highly unlikely that lower income groups would benefit from scrapping even a very pro-rich service. However, if the money were used to pay for other more pro-poor services, then clearly lower income groups would benefit as a result.

Developments on previous work

Previous work in this area has produced two conflicting stories about the distribution of benefits from welfare services. On the one hand, the government's own analysis (by the Office of National Statistics) suggests that poorer income groups are doing significantly better than richer ones from the provision of these services. The Office of National Statistics (formerly the Central Statistical Office) produces annual estimates of benefits in kind for health care, education, housing, and transport. Their analysis for 1993 showed that the value of benefits in kind received by the bottom quintile group was £3,610 per household, compared to £2,070 received by the top quintile group. However, their methodology is a fairly crude one. For example, the estimates for health care use a simple age/sex breakdown, which ignores other influences on the use of health services, including people's income. Nor do the Office of National Statistics (ONS) figures allow us to examine changes in the value of benefits in kind since 1979, partly because the estimates were never designed to be a fully consistent series and partly because the way in which their results are presented was substantively altered in 1987.

The picture painted by the ONS contrasts with earlier analysis by Le Grand in *The Strategy of Equality* (1982), which argued that the better-off were getting more than their fair share and that the welfare state had failed in achieving its redistributive role. Various reasons were put forward as to why richer, middle class, people were 'capturing services'. For example, poorer people may face higher costs in using services, because they have less access to cheaper forms of transport and because they may be more likely to lose pay if they are forced to take time off. It was also suggested that middle class patients managed to get more from the NHS, because they were more articulate and because they had more in common with their doctors than working class patients. However, the book was not always addressing the same questions as the ONS. For example, Le Grand did not argue that richer people were receiving more health care, but that they were getting more treatment *in relation to their need* than the poor. His analysis included tax expenditures (e.g. to owner-occupiers), whereas the ONS dealt strictly with public spending in the accounting sense. Subsequent analysis has also questioned the methodology used by Le Grand and the representativeness of the year for which his analysis was carried out.

A more recent study carried out by Evandrou, Falkingham, Hills and Le Grand (1992) sought to produce more accurate estimates of benefits in kind for one particular year, 1987. Welfare expenditure was apportioned in line with people's actual use of certain public services using microdata from the General Household Survey, which is a representative sample of all households in Great Britain. The advantage of this over the methodology used by the ONS is that it is more sensitive to variations in the use of public services that are related to other, non-demographic, factors. This project builds on this work, developing the methodology further and applying it to three separate years covering the period 1979-93. The report addresses a number of problems associated with this kind of analysis. Where relevant, the

11

limitations of the ONS's analysis are highlighted, because their estimates represent the status quo.[1]

i *Comparability over time*

Since the aim is to examine *changes* in the distribution of benefits in kind, one of the main priorities was to ensure that methods and definitions were consistent over time. In some cases, this meant simplifying the methodology to one that was applicable in each of the years examined. For example, it was not possible to allow for the differential use of private health care, because sufficient information was not available in later years. This consideration also had an influence on the choice of services to be included in the analysis. The "Right To Buy" scheme was included, because any assessment of changes in housing subsidies during the 1980s would be incomplete if it did not take into account the sale of large numbers of council houses at heavily discounted prices.

ii *Benefits included*

In order to apportion the value of benefits in kind, it has to be possible to allocate benefits to individual people or households. This rules out public goods such as defence, law and order. If we include the value of cash benefits, which are already included in official measures of income, the ONS analyses allocate around 55% of government expenditure. This still leaves the other 45% unaccounted for, although a similar proportion of the taxation (or borrowing) used to finance this expenditure is also unallocated.[2] In this report the coverage of benefits in kind is extended to include Personal Social Services, as well as those services included in previous analyses (the NHS, state education, and council housing). Although it does not account for a significant amount of additional expenditure, PSS spending has a disproportionate impact on the distribution of benefits in kind - both by age group (because it is concentrated on the elderly) and by income group (because much of it is means-tested).

Of course, the existence of a benefit in kind does not require a concomitant amount of public expenditure. The sale of council houses at less-than-market value represents a clear subsidy to purchasers, but

---

1   The ONS analysis is not designed to answer detailed questions about who is benefiting from the provision of specific welfare services, so its limitations are judged against a standard it was not intended to achieve.

2   The main items of unallocated financing are government borrowing, employers' NI contributions, some expenditure taxes, and corporation tax.

does not require direct expenditure by government.[3] Similarly, renting out public housing at less-than-market rents involves a continuing subsidy to council tenants, even though the cost of building those properties may have been borne a long time ago. This analysis takes into account some, though by no means all, of these less direct forms of subsidy. A limitation of the ONS analysis is that it is designed to fit in with the national accounting framework and so it seeks to allocate current year expenditure only, which is not always a good measure of benefits in kind.

People also receive benefits in kind from their employers and from past investments, most obviously the imputed rent on owner-occupied housing. If we are strictly concerned with examining changes in people's standards of living, then we would want to include all forms of benefits in kind, regardless of the source. This report is concerned with the redistributive impact of the welfare state, but we hope to add analysis of the impact on the income distribution of including imputed rents to owner-occupiers in later work.[4]

iii Price adjustment

A particular difficulty in making comparisons over time is how to control for the effects of inflation. The most straightforward way is to use a general price index such as Retail Price Index (RPI). But the RPI is based on the prices of a bundle of goods and services that does not include welfare services, so it may not be very appropriate for adjusting the value of benefits in kind if the cost of these services has changed in relation to other goods.

An alternative would be to use a service-specific price index, such as the NHS Pay and Prices index. Service-specific or "own price" indices

---

3   In fact, the immediate impact of sales is to raise revenue, although this has to be offset, in the longer run, against the loss of foregone rental income and the possible cost of providing replacement social housing in the future.

4   A measure of income that includes 'housing income' gives a better indication of people's standard of living. In particular, it avoids distortions between tenures. The HBAI 'Before Housing Costs' definition of incomes does not allow for the fact that an outright owner will have a better standard of living than a tenant or a mortgagee who has the same income and is living in similar accommodation. The 'After Housing Costs' (AHC) definition of income does not adequately address this problem because it does not take into account differences in the quality of the housing people are living in. For example, a rich person who is living in a mansion (and has high housing costs) might have the same AHC income as a less well-off person who is living in a small flat (and has low housing costs), even though their standards of living are very different.

measure changes in the cost of providing a particular service, including, say, changes in doctors' salaries and/or the cost of drugs. If health care expenditure rises because doctors' pay has gone up, this increase would automatically be discounted by the use of an own price index. This, however, does not allow for any improvements in productivity; doctors may be getting paid more, but they may also be offering a better service.

In practice, RPI-adjusted expenditure will tend to over-estimate the growth in the value of benefits in kind, because public services are relatively labour-intensive and earnings have risen faster than the cost of other inputs. Own price-adjusted expenditure (or "volume terms" spending), on the other hand, will tend to produce under-estimates, because it ignores improvements in productivity. The truth probably lies somewhere between the two, but it is difficult to know exactly where without more information on productivity growth in the public services. All baseline results in this report are calculated using the RPI. Sensitivity analysis is carried out using own-price indices.

iv *Adjusting for needs*

If we are interested in the financial impact on individuals of the way spending on welfare services is funded and allocated, then there is no need to adjust for needs. What matters is how much better (or worse) off someone is with the provision of free health care or free education than they would be without these 'in kind' benefits (taking into account the effect on their tax bill). If, on the other hand, the question under examination is the impact of welfare services on *standards of living*, it may be inappropriate to add in the value of public services without also adjusting for the need for such services. The fact that 85-year olds are heavy users of the NHS does not make them "better off" than younger people, who have a much lower level of medical need. This suggests that "final income", as reported by the ONS, may not be a very good guide to relative living standards. An ideal measure would add estimated health benefits, but deduct estimated health needs. This is not practical because of the difficulties of measuring need. But, if this could be done, the resulting measure would probably not be very different from cash incomes, given that most public services are (at least in principle) delivered freely on the basis of need.

Although we cannot do much to adjust for differences in need between people in a given year, it is possible to adjust for changing needs over time, in particular the effects of demographic change. Individuals' use of (and need for) services is often strongly related to their age and gender. Changes in the demographic composition of the population can therefore have a significant impact on the distribution

14

of public expenditure, even if the welfare system itself does not change. By controlling for demographic factors, we can distinguish the effect of changes in the age and gender composition of the population (or particular income groups) from other effects, including changes in policy. The method for age/gender standardisation is described in Appendix 1. (Of course, age and gender are not the only determinants of need, so we cannot make a complete adjustment for changing needs. Changes in diet or lifestyle, for example, may affect people's need for health care.)

v Non-household population

A significant limitation of household surveys is that they omit people living in communal establishments. This would not matter if the use of public services by the "non-household" population were similar to that of the household population. On the contrary, these people are often the most intensive users of these services. They include people in residential homes, long-stay hospital patients, and students living in halls of residence. To ignore them would mean that a significant amount of public expenditure could not be allocated.

The approach taken in this report is to allocate some, or all, of this expenditure to the household population. In the case of health care, the rationale is that people benefit from having certain services available to them, even if they are not actually using them. Put differently, if people had to insure themselves privately for a package of care equivalent to that provided by the NHS, their insurance premiums would allow for the possibility that they might require long-term medical care. In the case of higher education, expenditure on non-resident students is allocated to parents. The justification for doing this is that in the absence of public subsidies, it is parents who would bear some, perhaps most, of the costs of educating their children.

vi Method of apportioning benefits

As explained earlier, ONS estimates of benefits in kind are based on standard additions depending on household composition. However, we know from other sources that the use of welfare services varies with factors other than age and gender. Allowing for factors like the differential use of private education and variations in the use of services with income has significant effects on the resulting picture. Our methodology is refined in other ways too. For example, adjustments are made for differences in the cost of treating different patients and the fact that some patients pay charges. A more sophisticated technique is also used to estimate the value of housing subsidies.

vii *Unit of analysis*

Previous analyses (including the ONS's) have examined the distribution of benefits in kind between *households*, giving the same weight to a single pensioner as to a family of five. This can have perverse effects on the distribution, which will be affected by differences in average household size between income groups, and by changes in household composition over time. In this report, the chosen unit of analysis is the individual, giving equal weight to each person as opposed to each household. This has the added advantage of being consistent with the DSS's official Households Below Average Income series, which gives equal weight to each individual in examining the distribution of cash incomes.

One problem in attempting to allocate benefits to individuals is that some benefits in kind, in particular housing, are shared by households. The value of these benefits of kind could be presented on a simple per capita basis, but this would ignore the existence of economies of scale. Instead, we make use of the official "McClements equivalence scale", which is used to adjust cash incomes for differences in household size (and composition). Although the McClements scale was not designed for equivalising housing benefits in kind, it seems preferable to allow for scale economies in some way than to ignore them completely. (Other public services, for example free health care, are not shared by households and so the value of these benefits in kind do not need to be equivalised.)

viii *Explaining distributional changes*

An important extension to previous analyses is an attempt to account for observed changes in the distribution of the social wage. This is important for several reasons. Firstly, it enables the significance of different effects to be put in context. How important, for example, were changes to the generosity of student grants relative to other changes in the funding of higher education? A second reason is that it affects our interpretation of the results. If, for example, there were a pro-rich shift in the distribution of health care services, then it clearly matters whether this is because elderly people (who need more health care) are moving up the income distribution or because fewer resources are being directed at poorer people of all ages. In one case, a policy response is probably not merited but in the other it probably is. Thirdly, it may uncover important effects that are otherwise obscured, because they have cancelled each other out over a particular period. For example, a fall in expenditure per student may be offset by an increase in the number of students. Where possible, our analysis seeks to disentangle these various effects.

Methodology

This section provides a brief description of the methodology used to apportion the social wage, which is summarised in Box 1. More details of how benefits in kind are allocated for each service are provided in subsequent chapters (see also Appendix 1).

The basis for our analysis is the information contained in two household surveys, the Family Expenditure Survey (FES) and the General Household Survey (GHS), which are representative of all households in the United Kingdom and Great Britain respectively. The FES provides detailed data on people's incomes, from which the official measure of income distribution, the Households Below Average Income (HBAI) series, is derived. We use HBAI net equivalised incomes (Before Housing Costs) to rank *individuals* by income group. The FES also contains other useful information, for example on rental payments. The GHS provides microdata on the use of certain public services, for example on the number of in-patient stays or GP consultations. A third data set, the Building Society Mortgages 5% sample, is used to estimate the value of council properties, which is the basis for calculating housing benefits in kind. Survey data are supplemented, where necessary, by other official sources. Government publications provide a breakdown of public expenditure by type of service. Other data not contained in household surveys, for example on admission rates to residential homes, are also taken from official publications.

Following other studies in this area, the value of benefits in kind from health care, education, and personal social services is measured by the amount of public spending on each of these services.[5] Expenditure is distributed between individuals according to their

---

5   This is not without its problems. It assumes, for example, that the value to the person receiving a service is equal to the cost of providing it. But if it costs nothing to see your GP, then people may go for very trivial matters with little benefit to themselves but at a much higher cost to the taxpayer. Equally, if hospital treatments are rationed, the value of an operation to waiting patients could well exceed its cost.

expected use of particular services, based on demographic and social characteristics (such as age, gender, and tenure), as well as income.

Box 1: Methodology

Income measure:	the measure of income, except where stated, is net equivalised income (before housing costs) using the definition from the DSS's Households Below Average Incomes series.
Equivalisation:	cash incomes and housing benefits in kind are adjusted for differences in household size using the McClements equivalence scale (see Appendix 1).
Income groups:	people are ranked into five income groups (or quintile groups) on the basis of net equivalised household incomes.
Unit of analysis:	the unit of analysis is the individual, so there are an equal number of people in each income group (as opposed to an equal number of households).
Price adjustment:	most figures are given in real terms (in 1993 prices) using the Retail Prices Index to inflate spending in earlier years; figures in 'volume terms', where presented, are calculated using service-specific price indices (e.g. the NHS Pay and Prices index).
Method of allocating benefits in kind:	in most cases, expenditure is allocated according to people's expected use of services, based on demographic and social characteristics, as well as income; in the case of housing, benefits in kind are based on a measure of the economic subsidy to council tenants and Right To Buy households.
Non-household population:	spending on the non-household population is taken into account by allocating to people an actuarial 'insurance' premium for these services (e.g. for residential care, this would be based on the probability of them entering a home).

In the case of housing, however, public expenditure in any given year is a poor guide to the value of benefits in kind. Once a stock of properties has been built, they provide a flow of services to their occupants, which cannot be properly assessed by examining current expenditure on those properties or capital expenditure on new properties. Thus, an alternative approach is used, which attempts to measure the flow of benefits (or the economic subsidy) from public housing. This is described further in Chapter Four).

Chapter Two: Overall Changes in the Distribution of the Social Wage

The current distribution

Figure 2.1 shows the distribution of benefits in kind in 1993, based on the methodology described in Chapter One. Estimates are presented by quintile group, ranked on the basis of people's net (equivalised) cash income. The distribution of these benefits was fairly pro-poor in the sense that lower income groups received a greater absolute value of benefits in kind than higher income groups. In fact, the average value of benefits in kind received by people in the bottom quintile group is about 70 per cent greater than for the top quintile group. However, there is a slight hump in the distribution. As we shall see later, this is partly explained by demographic factors, in particular the high proportion of retired households in the second quintile group.

Health care and education are clearly the largest components of the social wage, together accounting for well over 80 per cent of the total. However, housing and personal social services have a very significant distributional impact, because these services are more closely targeted at poorer income groups.

For comparison, the Office of National Statistics (ONS) estimates of benefits in kind are presented in Figure 2.2.[6] These estimates are not directly comparable to ours, because their quintile groups are ranked by households, as opposed to individuals. However, there is a great deal of similarity in the shape of the two distributions. The ONS allocates a greater value of health care benefits to all income groups (probably because we do not apportion all NHS spending), but a smaller value of education benefits, especially to higher income groups; the latter is most likely explained by the different treatment of higher education.[7] The ONS's estimates of housing benefits in kind are also much lower than ours, partly because they ignore the Right To Buy Scheme and partly

---

6   The ONS's estimates are usually presented on a per household basis. These have been converted to a per capita basis by dividing by the average number of persons in each household by income group.

7   The ONS does not allocate spending on students who are living away from home. In this report, the benefits to 'non-resident' students are apportioned to parents.

Figure 2.1: Distribution of the Social Wage, 1993

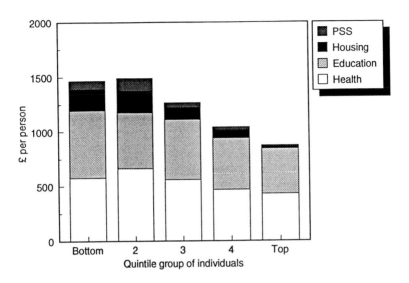

Figure 2.2: ONS Estimates of the Social Wage, 1993

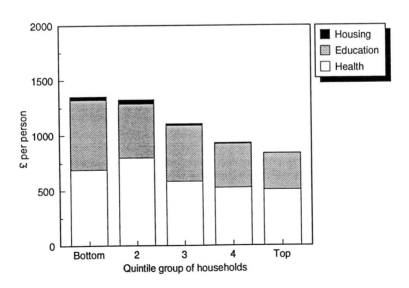

because we use a different methodology for measuring housing benefits in kind (see Chapter Four).

Returning to our own estimates, a useful distinction to make is between people living in retired and non-retired households, because their needs for health care, personal social services, and education differ so markedly (see Figure 2.3). Looking at non-retired persons only, the hump in the distribution disappears and the distribution is now consistently pro-poor. The distribution of health care spending is almost flat, but the distribution of education spending is strongly pro-poor. This is because lower income groups contain more children and more elderly people than other income groups. Since elderly people benefit very little from education spending, their removal accentuates the slope in the distribution of education spending.

The average value of benefits in kind received by retired people is higher than for non-retired people - by about a third. However, the shape of the distribution is different. Retired people in the middle income group receive more health care than other income groups, while those in the second quintile group receive the greatest value of housing and PSS benefits in kind. (The distribution of benefits from individual services is discussed in more detail in subsequent chapters.) This produces a hump-shaped distribution for retired persons, which is one reason why the distribution for the whole population is slightly hump-shaped. The other reason is that the second quintile group contains a greater proportion of retired persons than other income groups.

Importance of demographic and social characteristics

The distribution of the social wage can be looked at in different ways. An understanding of how the value of benefits in kind varies with other characteristics, such as age or family type, is interesting in its own right. It also helps towards understanding the distribution between income groups.

By age group

The distribution by age group is clearly U-shaped (see Figure 2.4). Children receive the majority of benefits from education and the elderly benefit most from health care and personal social services. The significance of PSS spending for the very elderly is particularly noticeable.

Figure 2.3: Distribution of the Social Wage between Non-Retired and Retired Persons, 1993

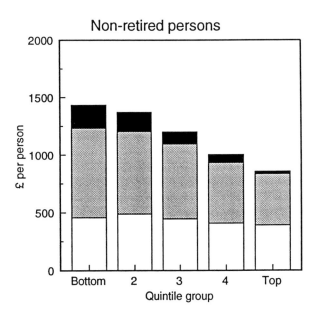

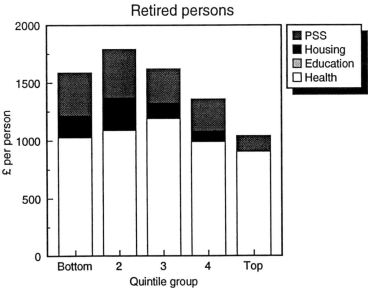

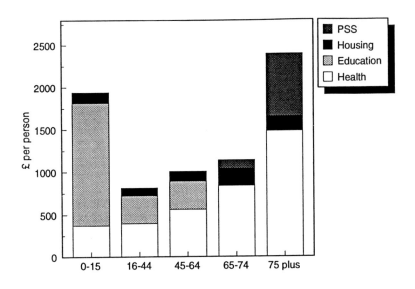

Figure 2.4: Distribution by Age Group, 1993

Figure 2.5: Distribution by Family Type, 1993

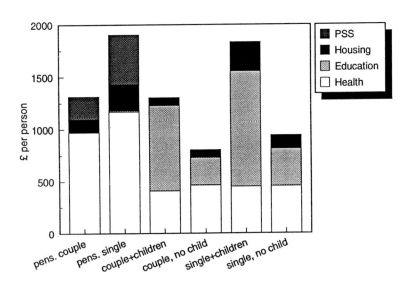

By family type

Not surprisingly, it is pensioners and persons living in families with children who receive the greatest value of benefits in kind (see Figure 2.5). Single pensioners do better than pensioner couples, probably because they are older on average, although their greater use of health care and personal social services may also be linked to them having less support at home. Members of single parent families receive more on average than other families because they contain a higher proportion of children and because they are more likely to be living in local authority housing.

By region

Regional variations in spending on health care and education mostly reflect differences in age composition (see Figure 2.6). For example, per capita spending on education is relatively high in Northern Ireland because it has the highest proportion of children of all the regions. (At this stage, no account is taken of regional variations in the unit costs of education and health care services, so these figures reflect differences in the use of services only.) The biggest variations between regions are for housing subsidies. These result from differences in the average value of properties, as well as the relative size of the local authority rented sector.

By tenure

Local authority tenants receive greater benefits in kind than people in other tenures (see Figure 2.7). Most, but not all, of the difference is due to the value of housing subsidies. The other three tenures receive about the same amount of benefits in kind. Owner-occupiers with a mortgage are younger than average, so they receive fewer benefits from free health care, and almost no benefits at all from personal social services. However, they also include more families than other tenures, and so have more spent on them on education; they also include beneficiaries of the Right To Buy scheme.

Impact on the income distribution

Figure 2.8 shows the effect of adding benefits in kind to the official HBAI measure of cash incomes. (This measure of "final" income is different from the ONS's definition of final income in that we do not deduct the value of indirect taxation.) On average, the social wage makes up just over one eighth of final income. However, it is a much greater

Figure 2.6: Distribution by Region, 1993

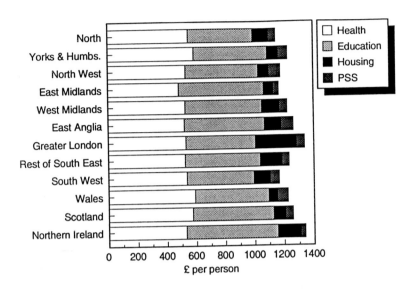

Figure 2.7: Distribution by Tenure, 1993

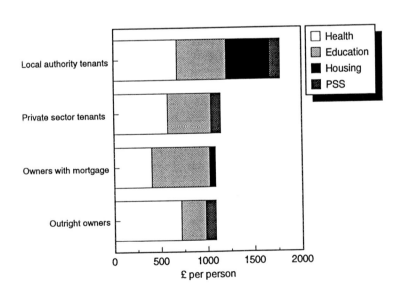

Figure 2.8: Distribution of Final Incomes, 1993

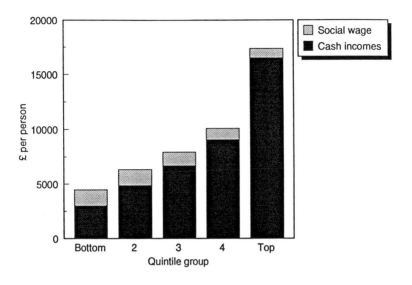

Figure 2.9: Share of the Social Wage in Final Income, 1993

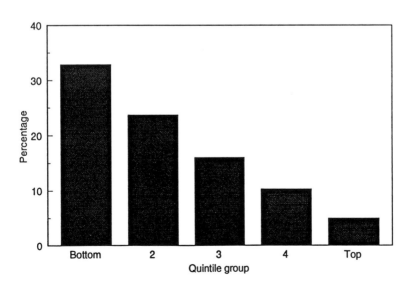

proportion of final incomes for people lower down the income distribution - around one third for the bottom quintile group (see Figure 2.9). This is partly because the social wage is worth more for people in lower income groups, but more important are the significant differences in cash incomes between income groups.

Even if the value of the social wage were the same, on average, across income groups, it would still have an equalising effect on final incomes. (To have no effect at all, benefits in kind would have to be as unequally distributed as cash incomes are.) One way to assess the equalising effect of the social wage is to look at the share of income received by each quintile group before and after the addition of benefits in kind (see Table 2.1 below). The effects are small, but unambiguous. The bottom three quintile groups receive a greater share of final incomes than of cash incomes, and vice-versa for the top quintile groups.

Table 2.1: Share of Cash and Final Income by Income Group (%)

1993	Bottom	2	3	4	Top
Cash income*	7.5	12.1	16.6	22.6	41.3
Final income*	9.7	13.7	17.1	21.8	37.7
Difference	+2.5	+1.6	+0.5	-0.8	-3.6

*   Net equivalised income.

Composition of the population

Before we go on to consider how the distribution of the social wage has changed since 1979, it is worth looking at changes in the composition of the population over this period, because these can have a significant impact on the distribution. As shown in Figure 2.4, the use of certain services is very sensitive to age. Other things being equal, spending on health care and personal social services increases with age, and spending on education decreases with age.

Figure 2.10 shows how the age composition of the population by income group has altered between 1979 and 1993. This reveals two significant demographic changes. Firstly, there was a large shift in the elderly population from the bottom quintile group to other quintile groups, particularly the second quintile group. Secondly, there was a significant reduction in the proportion of children in the population (from 26% to 23%) and also a shift in the position of the households they were living in from the middle of the income distribution to the bottom quintile group. The biggest net effect is that pensioners who were in the

Figure 2.10: Age Composition of the Population, 1979-93

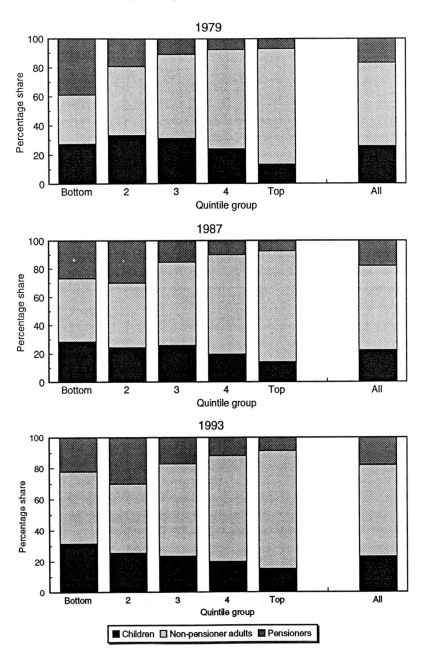

bottom quintile group in 1979 have effectively swapped places with families in the second quintile group.

Changes in the distribution of the social wage

Figure 2.11 shows how the distribution of benefits in kind has changed since 1979 and a summary of these results is provided in Table 2.2. There were some major changes over this period:

- the overall value of benefits in kind increased by around 30 per cent (in real terms).
- the second quintile group benefited more than others from this increase, changing the distribution from one that was consistently pro-poor to one that had a slight hump in it by 1993.

Table 2.2: Distribution of Benefits in Kind, 1979-93 (all persons, 1993 prices in real terms)

	Health	Education	Housing	PSS	Total
1979					
Bottom	530	360	170	50	1110
2	420	480	140	20	1060
3	350	490	130	10	980
4	340	420	100	10	870
Top	340	330	70	0	740
All	390	420	120	20	950
1987					
Bottom	550	500	260	70	1380
2	530	440	150	90	1210
3	440	500	120	30	1090
4	400	440	80	10	930
Top	340	370	50	10	770
All	450	450	130	40	1070
1993					
Bottom	580	620	200	80	1480
2	660	510	200	120	1490
3	560	550	110	50	1270
4	470	470	70	30	1040
Top	430	410	20	10	870
All	540	510	120	60	1230

Figure 2.11: Changes in Distribution of Social Wage, 1979-93
(1993 prices)

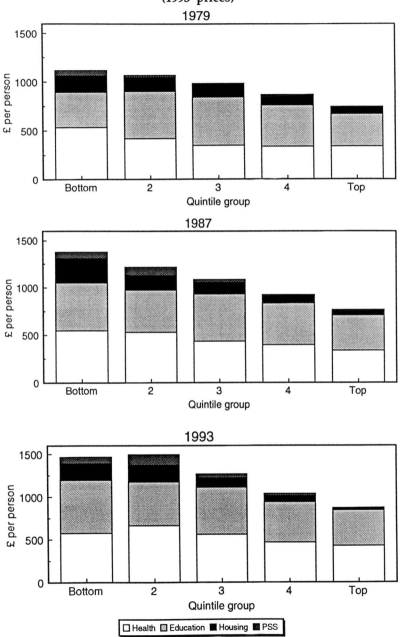

- the bottom quintile group experienced a large increase in education spending, but a much smaller increase in health care spending than other income groups. The opposite is true for the second quintile group.

- the value of housing subsidies remained almost unchanged on average, but with more going to those at the bottom of the income distribution and less to those at the top.

- the value of personal social services roughly trebled over this period. All income groups benefited, but the biggest increase was for people in the second quintile group.

A detailed analysis of these changes is reserved for subsequent chapters. However, it is worth emphasising the significance of the demographic changes discussed earlier. Much of the redistribution between quintile groups, especially the bottom two, can be accounted for by movements of elderly people and children between income groups.[8] Later in the report, we attempt to distinguish demographic effects from the other important changes that took place over this period.

Effect on trends in inequality

One of the aims of this report was to test the hypothesis that changes in the value of benefits in kind have helped to offset the growing inequality in cash incomes. There are two ways in which this could have occurred:

- a general increase in the share of benefits in kind in final income. We know from our analysis of the 1993 figures that the social wage is more equally distributed than cash incomes. Thus, a general increase in the size of the social wage in relation to cash incomes would have an equalising effect on final incomes, *even if the distribution of the social wage were unchanged;*

- a pro-poor shift in the distribution of benefits in kind. This would have an equalising effect on final incomes, *even if the average value of the social wage were unchanged.*

Of course, these two effects do not operate in isolation. If they are both working in the same direction, the first will magnify the second. and vice-versa. The first of the effects is easy to test. Whilst the overall

---

8   The results appear to be robust to the choice of equivalence scale. Using alternative equivalence scales affects the mix of spending on different income groups (between education and health care), but not the overall distribution of the social wage (see Appendix 2).

value of benefits in kind increased by 30 per cent between 1979-93, average cash incomes (BHC) rose by around 40 per cent. Thus, the value of the social wage actually *fell* as a proportion of final incomes from 14.0 per cent, on average, to 13.1 per cent.

The second of the above effects can be assessed by looking at the share of the social wage received by different income groups (see Table 2.3). The share received by the bottom quintile group rose (albeit marginally) and that of the second quintile group also rose (more than marginally), while the shares received by the top two quintile groups have fallen. This points to the distribution of the social wage being more pro-poor in 1993 than in 1979.

Table 2.3: Share of Social Wage by Income Group, 1979-93 (%)

Income group	1979	1987	1993	Change: 1979-93
Bottom	23.4	25.6	23.9	+0.5
2	22.4	22.6	24.3	+1.9
3	20.6	20.2	20.6	0
4	18.2	17.2	16.9	-1.3
Top	15.5	14.3	14.2	-1.3

The overall effect can be assessed by looking at changes in the shares of final income received by different income groups. From Table 2.4, it is clear that the top two quintile groups increased their share of final income at the expense of the bottom two quintile groups. Thus, changes in the social wage were not sufficient to prevent an increase in inequality between 1979-93. A more difficult question is whether the social wage had more of an equalising effect in 1979 than in 1993, in which case it could be argued that changes in its distribution offset *in part* the increased inequality in cash incomes. Since the two effects identified above are working in opposite directions, the answer is not clear cut.

A standard measure of income inequality is the Gini coefficient. Its value can range from zero - where everyone is receiving an equal income - to one - where one person is receiving all the income. Thus, a lower coefficient means a lower level of inequality. We know that benefits in kind have an equalising effect on incomes, so the Gini coefficient is lower for final incomes (which include the social wage) than for cash incomes (see Table 2.5).[9] The Gini coefficient for final income increased over this period, supporting the conclusion that changes in the social wage have not prevented inequality from rising. However, the coefficient for final incomes increased by less than the coefficient for cash incomes, suggesting that changes in the social wage have partly offset the increased inequality in cash incomes. This offsetting effect is fairly small, though, in relation to the overall change in cash income inequality (-0.019 compared to +0.093).

Table 2.4: Share of Final Income by Income Group, 1979-93 (%)

Income group	1979	1987	1993	Change: 1979-93
Bottom	11.9	10.8	9.7	-2.2
2	15.4	14.1	13.7	-1.7
3	18.4	17.5	17.1	-1.3
4	22.3	21.9	21.8	-0.5
Top	32.0	35.7	37.7	+5.7

Table 2.5: Measures of Income Inequality, 1979-93

Gini coefficients	1979	1987	1993	Change: 1979-93
Cash incomes	0.241	0.305	0.334	0.093
Final incomes	0.212	0.260	0.286	0.074
Social wage effect	-0.029	-0.045	-0.048	-0.019

An increase in the disparity of cash incomes between rich and poor might be less of a concern if all income groups were experiencing growing incomes. But, as Figure 2.12 shows, the cash incomes of those in the bottom quintile group (Before Housing Costs) rose only slightly between 1979-93, while those of the top quintile group rose by nearly 70 per cent.

If we include the value of the social wage, measured in real terms, the disparity between income groups remains, but the bottom income group does experience a more significant increase (13 per cent as opposed to 6 per cent for cash incomes). On this basis, it might be argued

---

9   Although, as already noted, final income is not necessarily a good guide to living standards, because it ignores the fact that some people have a greater need for welfare services than others (e.g. elderly people for health care).

Figure 2.12: Growth in Different Income Measures, 1979-93

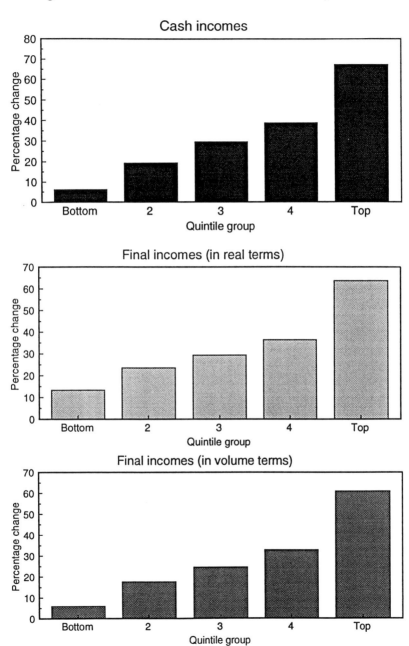

that people at the bottom of the income distribution have benefited more from economic growth than is normally recognised, as a result of increased spending on public services.

So far, however, benefits in kind have been measured in real terms using the Retail Price Index to inflate values in earlier years. This will tend to over-estimate increases in the value of benefits in kind, because the cost of providing welfare services has been rising relative to the general rate of inflation, which is what the RPI measures. Alternatively, benefits in kind can be measured in volume terms using service-specific price indices to adjust the value of benefits in kind (see Chapter One). Measured *in volume terms*, the final incomes of the bottom quintile group rose by just 6 per cent - no faster than cash incomes. Allowing for some improvement in the productivity of public services over this period, the actual growth in the final incomes of the bottom income group was probably somewhere between 6-13 per cent (the 'volume' and 'real' figures respectively). This is greater than the growth in cash incomes, but still considerably less than the increases enjoyed by higher income groups.

An important caveat to these results is that they do not take into account changing needs over the period. Changes in the age composition of the population, for example, will affect the overall need for welfare services, such as health care and education; they may also affect the relative needs of different income groups. Arguably, the ideal measure of final incomes should include an adjustment for needs. This might affect the conclusions of the analysis. If, for example, there has been a reduction in people's need for welfare services since 1979, then "needs-adjusted" final incomes will have risen faster than suggested in this chapter (and vice-versa).

As we have already seen, there was a fall in the child population which will have reduced the need for education, while increases in the elderly population will have increased the need for health care and personal social services.[10]. The *net* effect of demographic changes is unlikely to be sufficient to overturn our main conclusions with respect to the overall distribution of benefits in kind. Nevertheless, they may have had significant effects on the distribution of benefits from individual services. These are explored in the service-by-service analyses that follow.

---

10 Other changes over this period, for example the rise in unemployment, may also have affected the need for public services.

Summary

- The distribution of the social wage is pro-poor throughout the period, in the sense that lower income groups receive a greater absolute value of benefits in kind from welfare services than do higher income groups (see Table 2.2);

- The value of the social wage received depends to a large extent on demographic and social characteristics. Children and people aged over 75 receive the most benefits in kind (see Figure 2.4). Thus, changes in the demographic composition of the population will have a significant impact on the distribution of the social wage;

- Since 1979, the overall value of the social wage has risen by around 30 per cent. This is less than the growth in people's cash incomes (around 40 per cent), so the size of the social wage has fallen in relation to cash incomes;

- However, the distribution of the social wage did become slightly more pro-poor between 1979-93 in that the bottom two quintile groups were both receiving a slightly larger share of total benefits in kind at the end of the period (see Table 2.3);

- Overall, changes in the social wage did not prevent a rise in inequality, but they did help to offset the increased inequality in cash incomes. According to a commonly used measure of income inequality, the Gini coefficient, the rise in inequality between 1979-93 is lower by around one fifth once changes in the social wage are taken into account (see Table 2.5);

- Compared with 1979, the cash incomes of the bottom quintile group were only 6 per cent higher in 1993 (while those of the top quintile group were almost 70 per cent higher). If we include the social wage in our measure of incomes, the increase for the bottom income group was between 6-13 per cent (depending on how price inflation is adjusted for). Only to this limited extent, is it possible to argue that people at the bottom of the income distribution have benefited from economic growth through higher spending on public services (see Figure 2.12).

Chapter Three: Service-by-Service Analysis: Health Care

Background

A breakdown of expenditure on the National Health Service is provided in Table 3.1. These figures are adjusted to 1993 prices using the Retail Prices Index. They show a significant increase in total spending of 44 per cent between 1979-93, which is greater than the growth in GDP over the same period (around 30 per cent). The biggest increases were for Community Health Services (170 per cent), day patients (150 per cent) and out-patients (90 per cent). Spending on long-stay patients fell in real terms (by 10 per cent) as did capital expenditure (by 30 per cent). Charges for certain services rose very sharply over the period, although this was from a relatively small base.

One of the reasons there is so much debate about whether the NHS is being adequately resourced is that comparisons over time are very sensitive to the choice of price index (Hills, 1993). The costs of medical staff and equipment have risen faster than other goods and services in the economy. If we allow for this by using the NHS's own Pay and Prices Index, the increase in NHS spending is far less dramatic - just 10 per cent in 'volume terms'. On top of this, demographic change, in particular an ageing population, is putting more pressure on the health care system. Needs-adjusted expenditure has risen by even less over the period.

It is against this background that we attempt to explain changes in the distribution of health care expenditure. To what extent can any changes be attributed to purely demographic factors? Have changes in the balance of spending between health services had unintended distributional effects? What has been the impact on the distribution between income groups of attempts to redistribute resources between regions and to focus more spending on 'priority' groups, such as the elderly? Who has borne the brunt of higher charges?

Methodology

Over 90 per cent of expenditure on the National Health Service is allocated. Most of this is distributed to individuals in proportion to their expected use of different health care services, using microdata from the General Household Survey. Some adjustments are made for differences in the average cost of treating patients. For example, older patients are generally more expensive to treat. Charges are then deducted for patients who are not exempt from them. At this stage, no account is taken of regional (or sub-regional) variations in the unit cost of health care services. In other words, an in-patient stay or a GP consultation is assumed to cost the same throughout the United Kingdom. In practice, unit costs are likely to vary between regions and within regions. The potential distributional impact of local variations is examined in Chapter Seven.

Table 3.1: Expenditure on the National Health Service*, 1979-93
(current expenditure, £ million, 1993 prices)

	1979	1987	1993	% change: 1979-93
Hospital and Community Health Services				
In-patients (short stay)	8076	9038	12207	51
In-patients (long stay)	2679	2770	2412	-10
Out-patients	1899	2420	3571	88
Day-patients**	173	247	430	149
Community health services***	1404	2235	3783	169
Total	**14230**	**16709**	**22403**	57
Family Practitioners				
GP consultations	1468	2069	2297	56
Prescriptions	2428	3063	3339	38
Dental services	843	951	1020	21
Opthalmic services	194	246	224	15
Total (gross)	**4933**	**6330**	**6880**	39
Charges	431	684	761	76
Total (net)	**4502**	**5646**	**6119**	36
Other current***	3776	3707	3750	-1
Total National Health Service				
Current	21535	25342	32033	49
Capital	1404	1405	999	-29
Total	**22939**	**26746**	**33032**	44

*   breakdown of expenditure by service is based on England figures only;
**   expenditure not allocated;
***   expenditure on "other community health services" and "other hospitals" is not allocated, totalling around £2.5 bn in 1993.
Sources: DoH (1995a); Welsh Office (1994); Scottish Office (1996).

For the sake of consistency, all treatments are assumed to be on the NHS, because the GHS does not make a distinction between private and NHS treatment in all of the years examined. This does not affect the average value of benefits in kind (which is tied to total NHS spending), but it will affect the distribution, because the use of private health care varies between income groups. Sensitivity analysis in Appendix 3 suggests that taking the differential use of private health care into account would produce a more pro-poor distribution of benefits, but that the impact is not particularly significant.

Survey data are not available on the use of certain services (for example dental care and most community health services), so these are distributed on a simple age/sex basis using Department of Health data. Nor can spending on long-stay patients be allocated using survey data, since these patients will not be captured in household surveys (as discussed in Chapter One). Expenditure on the non-household population is allocated separately using an age and gender breakdown of resident psychiatric and geriatric patients. The implication of allocating some NHS spending (around 10 per cent of the total) on a simple age/sex basis is that the resulting distribution will not fully reflect variations in the use of services that are related to people's income. Further details of the methodology are provided in Appendix 1.

The distribution of health care spending

Estimates of the distribution of health care benefits in kind are given in Table 3.2 and illustrated in Figure 3.1 below. This shows that the distribution for all people is pro-poor, which is what we would expect given the concentration of elderly persons at the bottom of the income distribution. The distribution becomes less pro-poor over the period, mirroring the shift in the elderly population from the bottom to higher quintile groups (see Figure 2.10).

It is evident from looking at the distribution for non-retired people that not all income groups have benefited equally from the general increase in health care spending. Retired people, as a group, have done proportionately less well than non-retired persons, although they still have more than twice as much spent on them as non-retired persons.

Table 3.2: Distribution of Health Care Benefits in Kind, 1979-93

	1979	1987	1993	Changes: 1979-93	
				£s	%
All persons					
Bottom	530	550	580	50	9
2	420	530	660	240	57
3	350	440	560	210	60
4	340	400	470	130	38
Top	340	340	430	90	26
All	390	450	540	150	38
Non-retired persons					
Bottom	340	430	460	120	35
2	330	380	490	160	48
3	300	360	450	150	50
4	310	360	410	100	32
Top	310	310	390	80	26
All	310	360	430	120	39
Retired persons					
Bottom	860	890	1030	170	20
2	810	910	1090	280	35
3	840	940	1190	350	42
4	750	870	990	240	32
Top	820	780	900	80	10
All	830	890	1060	230	28

Variations in the use of health care services

To understand what is going on, it is necessary to look in more detail at how the balance of spending has changed between different age groups, regions, income groups, and health care services.

By age and gender group

Age and gender are key determinants of the use of NHS services. Health care spending increases with age and is particularly high for those aged over 75. However, the average amount spent on the elderly has fallen in relation to spending on other age groups (see Figure 3.2). One explanation is the shift in the balance of spending on different services (see below). Another is that reductions in average lengths of stay (for

Figure 3.1: Distribution of Health Care Benefits in Kind, 1979-93 (in 1993 prices, real terms)

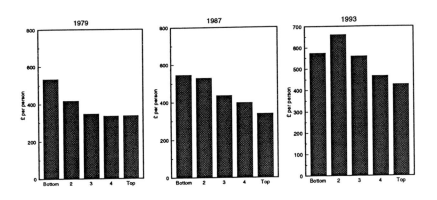

Figure 3.2: Value of Health Care Services by Age Group

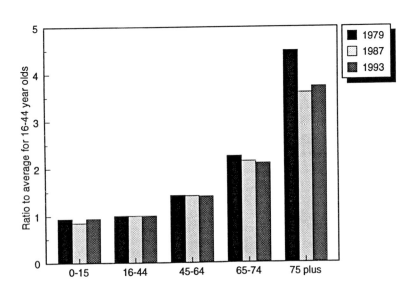

short-stay patients) have been greater for elderly patients (see Table 3.3 below).

Table 3.3: Average Length of In-Patient Stay,* 1979-93

Age group	0-4	5-14	15-44	45-64	65-74	75 plus
1979**	6.3	5.1	6.1	11.0	17.0	29.4
1993***	3.1	2.5	3.4	5.7	7.5	9.7
% change: 1979-93	-51	-51	-44	-48	-56	-67

*   short-stay in-patients only.
**   estimates based on Hospital In-Patient Enquiry, 1979-85 .
***   from Hospital Episodes Statistics.

The effect of gender varies significantly between age groups (see Figure 3.3). More is spent on women aged 16-44 than on men, primarily due to maternity and gynaecological services, but less is spent on women over 65 than on men of that age. This pattern has not changed significantly over the period, although slightly more is spent on very old men relative to very old women than was the case in 1979.

By region

The distribution of spending between regions is affected by differences in the demographic composition of their populations, as well as genuine differences in resourcing. To make the comparison fair, regional spending figures are adjusted for age and gender and compared to the national average. Looking at Figure 3.4, it is clear that there were large variations in the use of health care services in 1979,[11] which is why the Resources Allocation Working Party (RAWP) was set up in the 1970s to establish a more equitable distribution of NHS resources.

Between 1979-93, there was a significant shift in the balance of resources away from Greater London, which was receiving more than its fair share of health care spending, towards the North West and Yorkshire and Humberside, which were receiving less than their fair share. This supports previous analysis showing that RAWP has been effective in reducing, but not removing, regional inequalities in health

11   At this stage, our analysis assumes uniform unit costs across regions. Thus, Figure 3.4 is measuring differences in the use of health care services between regions, but not differences in unit costs by region.

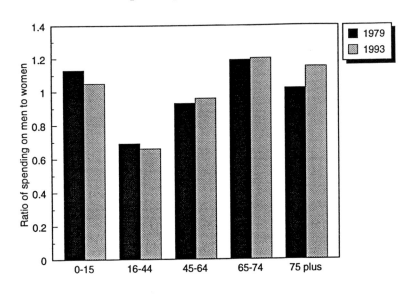

Figure 3.3: Value of Health Care Services by Gender (ratio of spending on men to women)

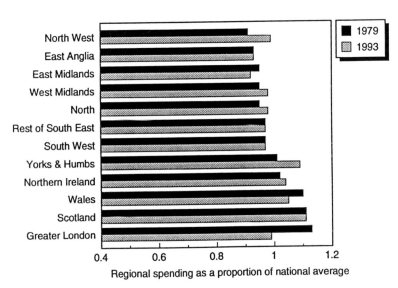

Figure 3.4: Value of Health Care Services by Region (after adjusting for differences related to age and gender)

care (Hills, 1990). However, RAWP only applies within England. Scotland, Northern Ireland, and Wales had, and still have, higher per capita expenditures than the average for England.

By income group

Of particular interest in this report is the relationship between the use of services and people's income. We know from previous research (O'Donnell and Propper, 1991) that, on average, poorer people are expected to make greater use of health care services. In addition, poorer people are more likely to be exempt from charges. Taking these factors into account should produce a more pro-poor distribution of health care benefits in kind. However, it is less clear how their inclusion will affect *changes* in the distribution over time.

Figure 3.5 shows how spending on different income groups has changed between 1979-93, *after adjusting for the effects of changes in age, gender, and region*. This shows that in 1979, poorer people in a given age, gender, and regional group received more health care than richer people. But, this picture changes by 1993. Spending on people in the second and third quintile groups increases relative to other income groups, including the bottom quintile. This is a further reason why the distribution of health care spending becomes hump-shaped in 1993, reinforcing the effects of demographic change.

By health care service

Figure 3.6 shows the decline in the proportion of NHS expenditure on long-stay hospital patients. One explanation is that the same patients are being discharged more quickly and indeed there was some increase in the share of spending on shorter-stay patients. However, a more important reason is the greater reliance on nursing homes (see Chapter Five). Community Health Services have almost doubled their share of total spending, in line with the policy to shift more resources towards primary care. The share of spending on family practitioner services has not increased, though, in part because of the effect of higher charges. The distributional impact arises from the fact that use of these different services varies between patient groups. For example, elderly people make up a disproportionate share of long-stay patients and so will have been hardest hit by the reductions in this service.

Figure 3.5: Use of Health Care Services by Income Group (after adjusting for differences related to age, gender and region)

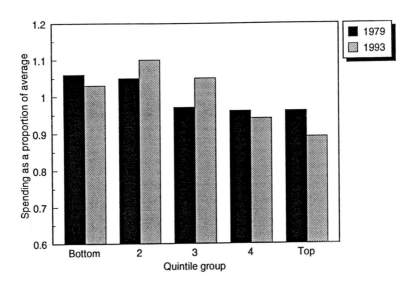

Figure 3.6: Distribution of NHS Spending between Services

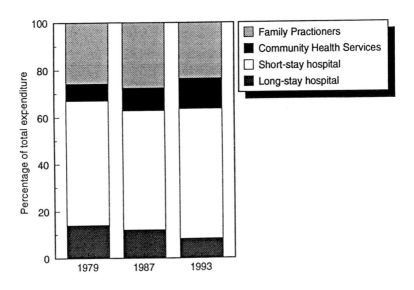

Unit costs of health care services

Changes in the overall level of spending can be split between changes in output and changes in unit costs (i.e. expenditure per unit of output). Table 3.4 shows how the output and unit cost of some health care services have changed since 1979. The distinction is useful, because at the end of the day it is changes in the output of services, including its quality, that matter. In practice, output is measured by the number of in-patients discharged, or the number of prescriptions issued, which does not capture changes in quality over time. Thus, an increase in unit costs could mean that it is costing more to produce the same standard of service, or it could mean that a better service is being provided. Again, the distinction is crucial, because changes in unit costs should only affect our estimates of benefits in kind if they represent a change in the quality of service being produced. (If unit costs are increasing because services are being produced less efficiently, then this should not be counted as an increase in the value of benefits in kind.)

Table 3.4: Output and Unit Cost of NHS Services, 1979-93

	In-patient stays	Out-patient stays	GP consultations	Prescriptions
Output (per person per year)				
1979	0.12	1.06	6.55	6.98
1993	0.17	0.92	8.92	9.70
% change	+36	-13	+36	+39
Unit cost (£ per unit of outout, 1993 prices)				
in real terms				
1979	1,598	33.40	4.17	6.78
1993	1,560	72.00	4.79	7.00
% change	0	+116	+15	+3
in volume terms				
1979	2,032	42.50	5.30	8.62
1993	1,560	72.00	4.79	7.00
% change	-23	+69	-10	-19

Ideally, we would like to measure how much of any change in unit costs can be explained by factors other than changes in quality. One such factor is that cost inflation was probably higher for health services than for other goods and services in the economy.[12] An obvious reason is that it is very labour-intensive and labour costs have tended to rise relative to other inputs. Table 3.4 shows the effect on unit costs of using the NHS Pay and Prices index, rather than the Retail Prices Index, to adjust expenditure figures. According to this, unit costs measured in 'volume terms' have actually fallen over the period for most services. Other things being equal, this would suggest that the quality of services has, if anything, declined. However, as mentioned earlier, the NHS Pay and Prices Index does not make any allowance for the fact that higher pay may reflect higher productivity, so it will tend to exaggerate cost inflation.

Charges

Charges have been raised sharply since 1979, not only on prescriptions but also on NHS dental treatment and eye care - for which eligibility for free care was severely restricted in 1987. An increasing amount of revenue has also been raised from charges for certain hospital services, such as amenity beds. Nevertheless, revenue from charges still represents a relatively small proportion of gross spending - 3.7% in 1992/3 compared to 2.3% in 1979/80.

Charges will fall hardest on higher income groups, because those groups who are exempt from them, including children, people over 65, and families of people on Income Support, are concentrated lower down the income distribution. Whilst charges have been rising, the proportion of people exempt has been rising. For example, the number of exempt prescriptions as a proportion of all prescriptions has risen from 65 per cent in 1979 to around 88 per cent in 1993. Thus, more revenue is being raised from fewer people.

Accounting for distributional changes

The main factors affecting the distribution of health care can be summarised as follows:

- demographic changes, in particular changes in the age composition of income groups;
- changes in the balance of services between age and gender groups, regions, and income groups;
- changes in unit costs;

---

12 Expenditure has already been adjusted for changes in general inflation using the Retail Prices Index.

- changes in charging policy;

The changes that have taken place since 1979 have already been discussed, but this did not examine the relative significance of their effects. Table 3.5 seeks to address this question by exploring what the distribution would have looked like if these changes had not occurred. The figures in Box A show actual changes in the value of health care benefits in kind by quintile group. As described earlier, it is the middle income groups that have benefited most from the increase in NHS spending and the bottom group that has benefited least. Boxes B and C measure the effect of individual factors on the distribution, in other words the difference between the actual distribution in 1993 and the distribution that would have resulted if a particular change had not taken place over the period. For example, how different would the distribution have been if the demographic composition of the population had not changed since 1979 or if unit costs had been the same as in 1979? The rows in Box B shows how much more (+) or less (-) each income group received in £s per person as a result of a particular change occurring. Box C presents the same results in a slightly different way. They show how significant the changes are in relation to total spending on that income group in 1993. This is useful for comparing the significance of effects across income groups. If the effects are proportional (i.e. the same percentage change for all income groups), then the distributional impact can be considered neutral.

Row 1 of Boxes B and C shows how important demographic changes are in explaining distributional changes between 1979-93. Changes in the age composition of the population between 1979 and 1993 led to lower health care spending on the bottom income group (by £105 per person) and higher spending on other income groups (by £79 per person in the case of the second quintile group). This is because there were fewer elderly people in the bottom income group than in 1979 and more elderly people in higher income groups (see Figure 2.10). In aggregate, NHS expenditure was £13 per person higher as a result of demographic changes (see the final column). This is a measure of the additional pressures on spending imposed by an ageing population. Though significant, demographic changes explain less than one tenth of the *overall* increase in health care spending over this period (but a much larger share of the distributional changes).

Row 5 measures the impact of increases in the use of health care services by age, gender, region, and income group. It is the middle income groups, in particular the second and third quintile groups, that have enjoyed the biggest increases in services. The value of health care

Table 3.5: Distributional Changes in NHS Expenditure

	Bottom	2	3	4	Top	All
			Quintile group			
A. Distributional changes						
(£ per person)						
1979	538	420	348	335	338	396
1993 (unadjusted)	579	666	562	469	429	541
Actual change, 1979-93:						
in real terms	41	246	214	134	91	145
% change	7.7	58.7	61.4	39.9	26.8	36.7
B. Explanatory factors						
(£ per person)						
1. Changes in age composition of population	-105	79	50	27	12	13
Changes in the use of services:						
2. By age/gender group	42	47	44	43	44	44
3. By region	6	-1	5	-1	-8	0
4. By quintile group	-18	37	33	-11	-33	2
5. Total	30	83	82	31	3	46
Changes in unit costs:						
6. In real terms	81	86	80	73	67	78
7. In volume terms	-38	-52	-35	-21	-19	-33
8. Increases in NHS charges	-3	-4	-6	-7	-8	-6
C.						
(as a % of 1993 expenditure)						
1. Changes in age composition of population	-18.1	11.9	8.8	5.7	2.9	2.3
Changes in the use of services:						
2. By age/gender group	7.3	7.1	7.9	9.1	10.2	8.1
3. By region	1.0	-0.2	0.8	-0.2	-1.9	0.0
4. By quintile group	-3.1	5.5	5.9	-2.4	-7.6	0.3
5. Total	5.2	12.4	14.6	6.5	0.7	8.5
Changes in unit costs:						
6. In real terms	14.0	13.0	14.2	15.6	15.7	14.4
7. In volume terms	-6.6	-7.8	-6.2	-4.5	-4.4	-6.1
8. Increases in NHS charges	-0.5	-0.6	-1.1	-1.6	-2.0	-1.1

benefits in kind received by the third quintile group is nearly 15 per cent higher than if the use of services had been the same as in 1979, while for the bottom income group the corresponding figure is just 5 per cent (see Box C). The top income group has experienced almost no increase in NHS services since 1979.[13]

Rows 2-4 provide a breakdown of the figures given in Row 5, distinguishing the effect of changes in the use of services by age/gender groups (Row 2) from the effect of changes in the regional distribution of health services (Row 3) and the effect of changes in the use of services by income group[14] (Row 5).

Row 2 shows that all income groups have benefited from an increase in the use of services by age and gender group. However, in percentage terms, the top two income groups have benefited more than others (see Row 2 of Box C). This is because there was a fall in spending on very elderly people (see Figure 3.3). Since there are more elderly people in the bottom half of the income distribution, this will have favoured higher income groups.

Row 3 shows the distributional effects of changes in the regional pattern of services since 1979. The bottom income group is slightly better off (by £6 per person on average) and the top income group slightly worse off (by £8 per person on average). Thus, changes in the regional balance of services benefited the poorest. One reason is that residents of Greater London, which experienced the biggest reduction in services relative to other regions, are concentrated at the top of the income distribution. The distributional effects are relatively small, though, compared to the significant changes in the distribution of services by region (see Figure 3.4).

Row 4 shows that changes in the balance of services by income group (after adjusting for age, gender, and region) favoured middle income groups. In distributional terms, this effect dominated other effects on the use of services (i.e. Rows 2-3). The second and third quintile groups received around 6 per cent more health care spending as a result and the top income group around 8 per cent less. However,

---

13 This does not reflect the greater use of private health care by the top income group, since survey data does not allow us to distinguish private and NHS treatments.

14 The effect of changes in the use of services by region are calculated after adjusting for differences related to age and gender. The effect of changes in the use of services by income group are calculated after adjusting for differences related to age, gender, and region. Thus, figures in Rows 2-4 can be added together to give the totals in Row 5.

it is difficult to explain this effect, because it picks up everything except for changes in the use of services by age, gender, and region. In particular, we cannot say how much of it is due to the effects of government policy and how much is due to changes in morbidity. Appendix 3 explores this issue in more detail.

Rows 6 and 7 examine the effects of changing unit costs, as distinct from changes in the use of services (or output). This shows how sensitive the results are to the choice of price index. In real terms, unit costs have increased significantly since 1979, which explains why the value of benefits in kind are much higher (by an average of £78 per person) if increases in unit costs are measured in *real terms*. But, in volume terms, unit costs have fallen. Thus, benefits in kind are lower (by an average of £33 per person) if unit costs are measured in *volume terms*. Changes in unit costs were not uniform across health care services (see Table 3.4). This might have had distributional effects, because the mix of services varies between income groups. In practice, the distributional impact was small in that the effects of changing unit costs were roughly proportional across income groups (see Rows 6 and 7 of Box C).

Finally, Row 8 estimates the impact of increases in NHS charges. The value of benefits in kind is £6 per person lower, on average, than it would have been if charges had not risen as a proportion of gross spending. Not surprisingly, people in higher income groups were most affected by the increases, because a smaller proportion of them are exempt from charges. Compared to other factors affecting the distribution of health care benefits in kind, the impact of higher charges is small.

Summary

- The value of health care benefits in kind increased by almost 40 per cent between 1979-93. Middle income groups benefited most from this increase and the bottom income group the least (see Table 3.2);

- Most, but not all, the distributional changes can be explained by demographic factors, in particular the shift in the elderly population (who make the greatest use of health care services) from the bottom to higher income groups. However, the shift in favour of the second and third quintile groups was accentuated by changes in the balance of services between income groups independent of those resulting from demographic change (see below);

- Since 1979, there has been a marked shift in spending away from the very elderly, although they are still the most intensive users of the NHS. This favoured higher income groups, which contain fewer elderly people. The most likely explanation is that more elderly people are being treated in nursing homes (which fall outside the NHS), rather than in NHS geriatric wards. This has further distributional implications, because, unlike the NHS, support for nursing home residents is means-tested (see Chapter Five);

- Between 1979-93, the regional balance of health care resources has changed significantly (see Figure 3.4). Regions that received a greater-than-average amount of NHS resources in 1979 (e.g. Greater London) have experienced a reduction in services relative to other regions, while regions that were receiving less-than-the-average amount of resources (e.g. the North West) have enjoyed relative increases. Thus, regional inequalities in health care have been reduced, but not removed. The impact on the distribution between income groups is small, however. The top group is slightly worse off as a result, because it contains a relatively high proportion of Londoners;

- In 1979, lower income groups made greater use of health care services, after adjusting for differences related to age, gender and region. But, since 1979, there has been a shift in favour of the second and third quintile groups (see Figure 3.5);

- While the output of health care services increased over the period, it is less clear what has happened to unit costs. Unit costs have risen in real terms, but fallen in volume terms. If we allow for some productivity growth, then unit costs have probably risen. This means that, compared to 1979, people are not just receiving *more* treatment, they are also receiving *better* or *more intensive* treatment. The impact of changes in unit costs was similar (in proportional terms) across income groups, so they had little distributional impact;

- Charges increased sharply over this period, but are still low in relation to gross spending. Not surprisingly, higher income groups were hardest hit by the increase in charges, although the size of the distributional impact is relatively small.

Chapter Four: Service-by-Service Analysis: Housing

Background

There were some major changes in housing policy over this period.
Most notable was the reduction in the size of the local authority rented
sector, which resulted from the sale of over one and a half million
council properties to sitting tenants and from a cut in capital spending
on new social rented housing (while the owner-occupied sector
expanded rapidly). The policy of promoting owner-occupation was
accompanied by sharp increases in local authority rents above the rate
of inflation. At the same time, house prices soared at the end of 1980s,
making property a more valuable asset than before. Spending on
maintenance and management of the local authority stock was also
considerably higher at the end of the period.

This chapter does not cover Housing Benefit payments or tax
relief on mortgage costs, both of which are already included in the
official HBAI definition of cash income. Thus, our measure of housing
benefits in kind should not be used *on its own* to assess the overall
distributional impact of housing policy over this period. For example,
much of the increase in local authority rents was returned to tenants in
the form of higher Housing Benefit payments. The net reduction in
housing subsidies (as a result of higher rents) is therefore smaller than
suggested by our measure of benefits in kind, especially for poorer
tenants. By the same token, however, changes in HBAI 'Before Housing
Costs' incomes exaggerate the growth in living standards of low income
groups because they omit the impact of higher rents.

Methodology

Changes in the overall value of housing subsidies are more difficult to
measure than for other services because current expenditure is a poor
guide to the value of benefits in kind. The biggest item of expenditure
is the Housing Revenue Account Subsidy to local authorities to cover
the difference between expected rental income and interest charges on
past borrowing. This depends to a great extent on the maturity of the
stock, which is largely irrelevant to any proper valuation of housing
subsidies. The other major item is a grant to the Housing Corporation
to subsidise the construction of new social housing. But, what we would
like to measure is not the initial capital investment, but the flow of
benefits in subsequent years. Nor does spending on schemes to promote

owner-occupation adequately measure the benefits to participants. The most important scheme by far, the Right To Buy, involves no direct public expenditure, but involves a very significant subsidy to buyers in the form of large discounts on the purchase price. Thus, a different approach is needed to housing than to other public services.

Local authority tenants benefit from two forms of subsidy. Housing Benefit is paid to tenants who cannot afford to pay the full rent, but this is a cash benefit which is already taken into account in our measure of cash income. The other form of subsidy is that rents are lower than the 'economic rent' defined as the level of rent that would need to be charged if local authorities were to cover their costs in full. To measure this subsidy, we need to estimate economic rents and then deduct the rents actually charged by local authorities.

Unfortunately, the private rented sector is too small and has too long a history of regulation to be used as a basis for estimating economic rents in the social rented sector. An alternative methodology used in this and previous studies (Hills, 1991a) is to calculate economic rents as a fixed proportion of estimated property values[15] plus or minus various adjustments for upkeep, depreciation, and expected capital gains[16]. The rationale is that the return on housing should be competitive with the return available on comparable assets, after allowing for the additional costs involved in managing rented properties. What this measures is the 'opportunity cost' to the public sector of holding and maintaining a stock of properties. While this methodology is conceptually robust, it does not lend itself to very precise estimates. We therefore present a range of estimates based on different assumptions about the required rate of return.

Right To Buy participants are not specifically identified in the Family Expenditure Survey. Therefore, various criteria are used to select households who are *likely* to have bought their home under the scheme. For example, they must have lived in the house for at least two years prior to purchase (i.e. the qualifying period) and the size of their mortgage should be low relative to the value of the property (because of the discount received). An estimate of the total value of subsidies for the RTB scheme is calculated using data on the total number of sales

---

15   Property values are trended to ensure that estimates of economic rents are not unduly affected by large swings in house prices over this period. This is done by adjusting average property values in each year in line with increases in average male earnings. The rationale is that *in the long run* house prices are linked to people's ability to pay, as measured by their earnings.

16   The precise formula is given in Appendix 1.

and average rates of discount. This is then distributed between households identified as possible beneficiaries of the RTB scheme in proportion to the estimated value of their property and the discount they would have been eligible for. Rather than allocating to them the full value of the subsidy in the year of purchase, this is annualised over time (using the same rate of return used in calculating economic rents for local authority tenants).

Subsidies to housing association tenants are not included in our estimates of benefits in kind because these tenants are not separately identified in earlier surveys. The significance of this omission is examined in Appendix 2. This shows that the effect of including subsidies to housing association tenants would be a small addition to the value of housing benefits in kind (of around 8 per cent on average), but with little impact on the distribution of these benefits. Since the proportion of housing association tenants has increased over the period, our estimates will slightly underestimate the value of housing benefits in kind in 1993 relative to 1979.

The distribution of housing benefits in kind

Estimates of the value of housing benefits in kind are given in Table 4.1 and illustrated in Figure 4.1 below. This shows that the distribution is

Figure 4.1: Distribution of Housing Benefits in Kind, 1979-93

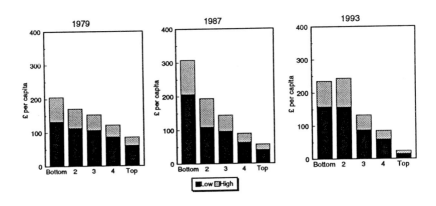

pro-poor in all three years. Between 1979 and 1993, the value of housing subsidies going to the top three quintile groups falls, while the amount going to the bottom two income groups increases. Thus, the distribution becomes more pro-poor over this period (although not since 1987). The biggest increase in subsidies is for the second quintile group.

Table 4.1 shows the distributions for non-retired and retired households separately. The value of benefits in kind going to retired persons has increased by an average of over 30 per cent , while for non-retired persons it has fallen by around 10 per cent. The most likely explanation is the increase in the proportion of local authority tenants who are retired (from 16.7 per cent in 1979 to 21.0 per cent in 1993).

Table 4.1: Distribution of Housing Benefits in Kind, 1979-93

	1979	1987	1993	Changes: 1979-93*	
				£s	%
All households					
Bottom	130-210	210-310	160-240	30	18
2	110-170	110-190	160-240	60	43
3	110-150	100-150	90-130	-20	-15
4	90-120	60-90	60-90	-30	-29
Top	60-90	40-60	20-20	-55	-73
All	**100-150**	**100-160**	**100-140**	**-5**	**-4**
Non-retired households					
Bottom	150-220	230-340	160-240	15	8
2	110-170	120-190	130-200	25	18
3	110-150	110-150	90-130	-20	-15
4	90-120	60-90	60-80	-35	-33
Top	60-90	40-60	20-30	-50	-67
All	**100-140**	**110-160**	**90-130**	**-10**	**-8**
Retired households					
Bottom	110-190	150-220	150-220	35	23
2	110-190	90-220	220-350	135	90
3	120-180	30-100	110-170	-10	-7
4	70-100	50-70	70-110	5	6
Top	60-80	20-40	10-10	-60	-86
All	**100-170**	**90-170**	**140-220**	**45**	**33**

*   Changes are calculated using the mid-point estimates for each year.

It may be surprising that the overall value of housing subsidies has not fallen more over this period, given the reduction in the proportion of local authority tenants and given the sharp increases in local authority rents. The reasons for this are explored in more detail below, but have to do with real increases in spending on maintenance and management, rising house prices, and the inclusion in our estimates of Right To Buy subsidies.

Changes in the shape of the distribution are a more complex phenomenon. The proportion of local authority tenants in each quintile group is obviously an important factor, but so are differences in the value of benefits in kind received by local authority tenant households. Higher rents clearly reduce the average value of housing benefits in kind, but have they hit some tenants harder than others? Who has benefited from the Right To Buy Scheme and by how much? These and other questions are addressed below.

Proportion of local authority tenants

Figure 4.2 shows how the proportion of local authority tenants and estimated Right To Buyers in each income group has changed between 1979-93. RTB households are counted, because they continue to receive

Figure 4.2: Distribution of Council Tenants and RTB Households

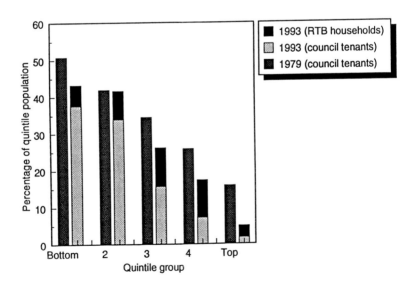

a subsidy, albeit in a different form. Overall, the proportion of beneficiaries fell from 34% of the population in 1979 to 27% in 1993. All income groups saw a significant reduction, except for the second quintile group. The reason for the overall reduction in the proportion of individuals in local authority tenant and Right To Buy households is that nearly all the increase in the stock of properties over this period was in other tenures, particularly the owner-occupied sector. The differences between income groups are harder to explain. Two factors provide at least part of the explanation:

- a fall in the average earnings of local authority tenants (and ex-tenants) relative to other tenures, possibly because public housing was more closely targeted at poorer households;

- as local authority rents increased so did Housing Benefit payments, pushing the incomes[17] of poorer local authority tenants above those of poorer owner-occupiers (even though they were no better off as a result).

The first of these would explain why local authority tenants and Right To Buy households are now more concentrated at the bottom of the income distribution. The second factor might explain why there was a shift of local authority tenants from the bottom to the second quintile group.

Average subsidies per tenant

While the proportion of local authority tenants and RTBers in the population fell, the average subsidy per tenant rose significantly in real terms between 1979-93 (although it was lower in 1993 than in 1987). In both years, tenants in higher income groups receive higher subsidies, on average, than tenants in lower income groups (see Figure 4.3). This agrees with earlier work by Evandrou et al. (1993).[18] However, the differences between income groups appear to have narrowed over the period as tenants in the bottom two quintile groups experienced greater increases in subsidies than other quintile groups. The reasons for this are complex, depending on changes in household size, rent levels,

---

17   Before Housing Costs.
18   Their explanation is that the differential in council rents between larger and smaller properties and those in high and low cost parts of the country is small relative to the differential in property values. Since tenants living in large properties and in high cost parts of the country are generally higher up in the income distribution, the average value of subsidies will be greater for tenants in higher income groups.

house prices, maintenance spending, and the impact of the RTB scheme. These factors are examined in turn:

Figure 4.3: Average Value of Housing Benefits in Kind by Income Group (beneficiaries only)

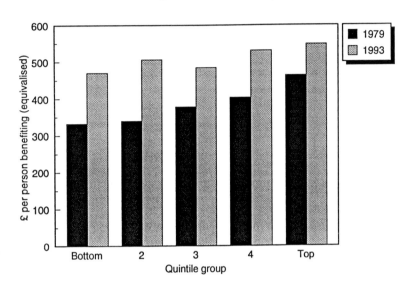

Household size

The average value of subsidies is very sensitive to household size (see Figure 4.4). Subsidies are higher for smaller households, because it costs more to house people in individual units than to house them together. A single person will generally occupy a smaller property than a family of four, but the difference in the value of their properties is unlikely to be as much as one-to-four.[19]

These differences are important, because there have been changes in the average size of local authority households. From Figure 4.5, it is clear that the average size of local authority households has fallen since 1979. More significant, though, is the difference between the bottom income group (slight increase) and the middle quintile groups (large falls). Other things being equal, the average subsidy to tenants in the

---

19 These differences are partly offset by using the McClements scale to equivalise housing benefits in kind, which allows for some economies of scale in the consumption of housing (see Chapter One).

bottom income group should have fallen relative to other income groups.

Figure 4.4: Average Value of Housing Benefits in Kind by Household Size (beneficiaries only), 1993

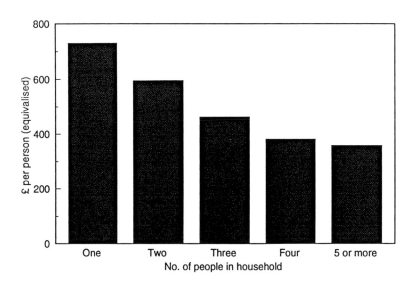

Local authority rents

Local authority rents have increased sharply since 1979 - by just under 80 per cent in real terms. Average rents went up by an average of 65 per cent for tenants in the bottom income group and by 155 per cent for tenants in the top income group. Thus, rent increases were to some extent targeted at richer tenants, especially those in the very top quintile group (see Figure 4.6). However, a significant proportion of better-off tenants will have avoided the effects of higher rents by purchasing their home under the Right To Buy scheme.

Property values

Our measure of the economic subsidy to local authority tenants is based on estimates of the value of the properties they are living in. It follows that an increase in house prices will lead to an increase in estimated benefits in kind. It is arguable whether rising house prices *should* count towards an increase in the value of housing benefits in kind. On the one

Figure 4.5: Average Size of Council Tenant Households

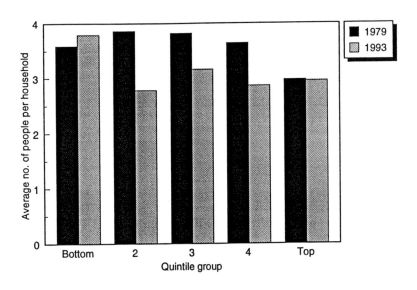

Figure 4.6: Average Local Authority Rent by Income Group

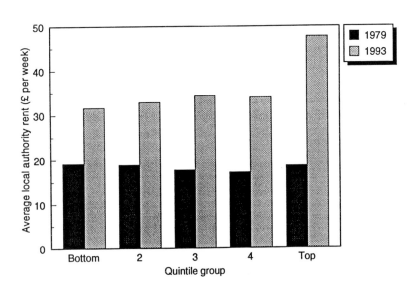

hand, tenants are occupying a more valuable asset than before. (In economic jargon, the opportunity cost of living in their home has gone up.) On the other hand, a house is a house, so why should the benefits to tenants be affected by changes in house prices? Of course, part of the increase in house prices may reflect genuine improvements in the quality of the stock, which should undoubtedly be included in the valuation of benefits in kind.

On average, the estimated values of council properties were around 30 per cent higher in 1993 than in 1979 (in real terms). This increase was driven by the general rise in *trend* house prices, which, in this analysis, is linked to male earnings. The value of local authority properties rose by less than house prices generally, because the more expensive properties were sold off under the Right To Buy scheme. Figure 4.7 shows how the average value of council properties increases as we move up the income distribution. Between 1979-93, values rose fastest for properties occupied by the richest tenants, accentuating the differential between the richest and poorest tenants.

Figure 4.7: Average Estimated Trend Value of Council Properties by Income Group

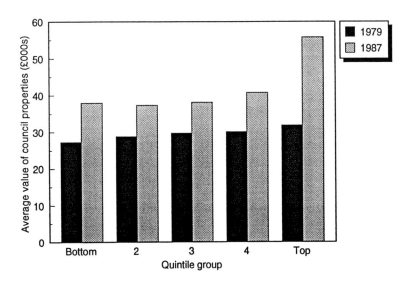

The combined effect of higher rents and higher property values is illustrated in Figure 4.8, which shows the *ratio* of annual rental payments to property values for tenants in different quintile groups. In 1979, the ratio of rents to property values is highest for the lower income groups, which explains why the average subsidy per tenant was also lowest for poorer tenants (see Figure 4.3). By 1993, the pattern has changed significantly. The ratio of rents to property values is higher for all income groups, but there is now little difference between tenants in different income groups. The smallest increase was for the bottom quintile group. This explains why subsidies to tenants in this income group rose relative to other income groups, in spite of the impact of changes in household size (see above).

Figure 4.8: Ratio of Council Rents to Property Values by Income Group

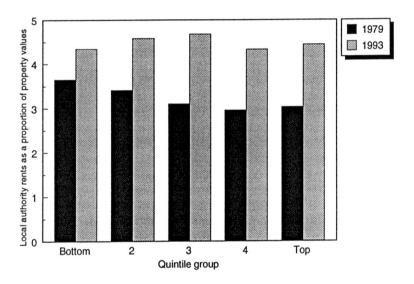

Maintenance and management spending

Real spending on maintenance and management (M&M) increased by an average of over 80 per cent between 1979-93. Figure 4.9 shows that there is little variation in spending between tenants in different income groups. The only change over the period is that tenants in the top quintile group enjoyed a slightly bigger increase in M&M spending than other income groups. However, while it is true that Right To Buyers did not suffer the effects of higher rents, nor will they have benefited from the increase in M&M spending.

Figure 4.9: Maintenance and Management Spending by Income Group

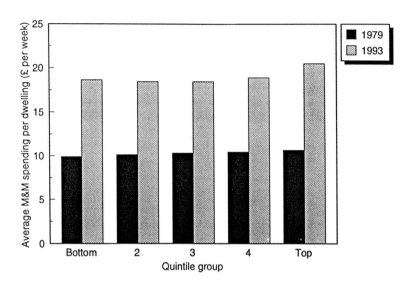

Again, it is arguable whether an increase in M&M spending should be counted as an increase in the value of benefits in kind. If local authority properties in one area are in particularly poor condition, should we be attributing to tenants the expenditure needed to restore them to a satisfactory condition? The answer depends on whether the poor condition of some council properties is reflected in lower estimated property values (and therefore lower economic rents). If the answer is yes, then it is reasonable to include M&M spending which aims to compensate for the poor condition of these properties.[20] Also, part of M&M expenditure is on other services to tenants than repairs related to worsened stock condition. Increases in this element of expenditure reflect a genuine improvement in benefits in kind.

---

20   The actual answer to this question is yes, but only to a certain extent. Estimates of council property values are based on the value of similar properties in the owner-occupied sector plus an adjustment for the fact that council properties are generally worth less than their counterparts in the owner-occupied sector (using information on the value of RTB properties). If the condition of RTB properties is better-than-average for the council stock (which it probably is), then our estimates are likely to overstate the value of the council stock.

Right To Buy scheme

Figure 4.10 highlights the significance of the Right To Buy scheme, particularly for higher income groups. However, the *net* effects of the Right To Buy scheme cannot be analysed without considering the value of the subsidies they have foregone as tenants. The economic subsidy each RTB household would have received if they had remained as tenants is estimated using data on rents and M&M spending for local authority properties of a similar size and in the same region. This is compared against the estimated value of the subsidy they receive under the RTB scheme.[21]

Figure 4.10: Value of Subsidies to Tenants and Right To Buy Subsidies, 1993

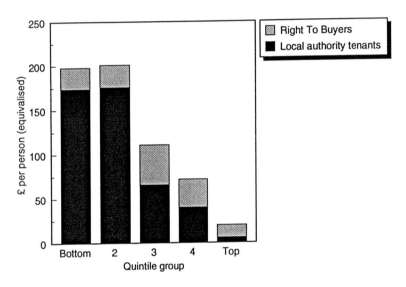

Interestingly, these calculations show that the average value of subsidies to Right To Buyers in 1993 is *less* than they would have received as local authority tenants. Box 4.1 provides an illustrative example for a fairly typical Right To Buy household. Although Right To Buy households receive a substantial discount on their property, they face additional costs, in particular maintenance and repair costs. Of course, these results are sensitive to the assumptions about the rents they would have paid as tenants and the amount local authorities would

---

21   See Appendix 1 for a description as to how this is calculated.

have spent on their properties. If, as seems likely, maintenance and repair costs for Right To Buy properties are lower than for comparable properties in the local authority sector, then Right to Buyers will be in a better position than suggested above. Nevertheless, it seems reasonable to conclude that the economic subsidies received by Right To Buy households are no higher, and probably lower, than they would have received as tenants.

Box 4.1: Net Effects of the Right To Buy Scheme

An illustrative example of the subsidy received by an RTB household compared to what they would have received as local authority tenants

Under the Right To Buy scheme:

Estimated current value of property:	£40,000
RTB discount:	47%
Imputed return on equity:	3.5 - 4.5%

Subsidy
=   Value of discounted equity x   Imputed return on equity
=   (50,000 x 47%)   x   3.5% or 4.5%
=   £820 - 1,060 per annum

As local authority tenants:

Estimated gross rent:	£34 per week
Estimated M&M spending:	£18 per week
Imputed return on equity:	3.7% - 4.7%
	(including 0.2% for structural insurance)

Subsidy
=   Imputed return on whole property   +   M&M spending - Gross rent
=   3.7% or 4.7% x 50,000   + £18 per week   - £34 per week
=   £1020 - 1,520 per annum

Of course, this could, and probably will, change over time. If, for example, local authority rents continue to rise as a proportion of property values then RTB households may be better off as they are than as tenants. The average discount rate on RTB properties has also been rising over time, again favouring the Right To Buy option. It is important to note that the estimates above ignore the non-pecuniary benefits of owner-occupation (e.g. freedom to make alterations to the property), which are known to be important in decisions to buy.

These calculations assume that Right To Buy households would have remained as local authority tenants if the RTB scheme had not been available. In practice, some of them would have left the local authority sector anyway, in which case any subsidy towards the cost of purchasing their own home represents a net benefit to the household.

Accounting for distributional changes

The main factors affecting the distribution of housing benefits in kind were:

- reductions in the proportion of local authority tenants (and Right To Buy households);
- changes in the average size of local authority tenant households by income group;
- increases in local authority rents;
- rising values of local authority (and RTB) properties;
- increases in maintenance and management spending per dwelling;
- the introduction of the Right To Buy scheme.

Table 4.2 analyses the impact of each of these factors on the distribution of housing benefits in kind. Box A shows what actually happened to the distribution of housing benefits in kind over the period 1979-93. There was little change in their overall value, but lower income groups received a larger share of the benefits than in 1979. Boxes B and C show how much more (+) or less (-) income groups received as a result of each of the changes identified above. For example, how much less did income groups receive because council rents have risen in real terms? The figures in Box B are given in £s per person. Box C presents the same figures as a proportion of the total value of benefits in kind received by each income group in 1993. This makes it easier to compare the proportional impact of changes on different income groups.

Row 1 of Boxes B and C measures the impact of changes in the proportion of people living in local authority housing and Right To Buy households. On average, this reduced the value of housing benefits in kind by £24 per person (or around 20 per cent). For all except the second income group, there were fewer people living in local authority housing or RTB households than in 1979 (see Figure 4.2). This explains a large

Table 4.2: Distributional Changes in Housing Benefits in Kind

	Quintile group					
	Bottom	**2**	**3**	**4**	**Top**	**All**
A. Changes in expenditure						
(£ per person)						
1979	169	142	130	105	73	124
1993	197	201	110	73	20	120
Actual change, 1979-93:						
in real terms	28	59	-20	-32	-53	-4
% change	16.5	41.4	-15.4	-30.5	-72.8	-3.0
B. Explanatory factors						
(£ per person)						
1. Changes in proportion of council tenants and RTBers	-24	3	-28	-30	-40	-24
2. Changes in average size of tenant households	-9	18	8	5	-2	4
3. Changes in local authority rents (in real terms)	-127	-166	-74	-34	-15	-83
4. Changes in trend property values (in real terms)	87	101	49	29	7	54
5. Changes in level of M&M spending (in real terms)	85	97	39	20	4	49
6. Introduction of Right To Buy scheme	-9	-5	-25	-13	-4	-11
C.						
(as a % of 1993 expenditure)						
1. Changes in proportion of council tenants and RTBers	-12.4	1.5	-25.4	-41.4	-200.0	-19.9
2. Changes in average size of tenant households	-4.4	8.9	7.3	6.6	-9.2	3.4
3. Changes in local authority rents (in real terms)	-64.6	-82.7	-67.2	-47.2	-76.1	-69.4
4. Changes in trend property values (in real terms)	44.0	50.2	44.2	39.3	37.5	45.3
5. Changes in level of M&M spending (in real terms)	43.3	48.1	35.7	26.9	21.8	40.8
6. Introduction of Right To Buy scheme	-4.3	-2.3	-23.0	-17.6	-22.2	-9.3

part of the reduction in benefits going to the top three quintile groups. It also helps to explain why the second quintile group experienced a bigger increase in benefits than the bottom income group.

Row 2 shows the impact of changes in the average size of households living in local authority housing. Compared to 1979, local authority tenants in the bottom income group were living in larger households, while the opposite is true of other income groups (see Figure 4.5). This matters because average subsidies per person are lower for bigger households. The bottom income group were slightly worse off (by £9 per person) and other income groups were better off (by £18 per person in the case of the second quintile group). This is a further reason why the second quintile group did better than the bottom quintile group. (The intuition behind this is that tenants in the bottom income group were having to share the benefits of subsidised housing between more people.)

Row 3 shows that increases in local authority rents had a substantial negative impact on the value of benefits in kind. Housing benefits in kind were lower by an average of £80 per person as a result of real increases in rents since 1979. Lower income groups were the worst affected in absolute terms, largely because they contain a greater proportion of people living in local authority housing (see Box B). However, in proportional terms, the impact across income groups is less clear-cut (see Box C). On the one hand, tenants in higher income groups experienced the biggest increases in rents (see Figure 4.6). On the other hand, many better-off tenants escaped the effects of higher rents by exercising their Right To Buy.

Row 4 measures the effect of rising property values on our measure of economic subsidy. People in lower income groups were the main beneficiaries, because a greater proportion of them were living in local authority housing, but in proportional terms the differences between income groups are much smaller. Right To Buy households also benefit from rising house prices, because the value of their subsidy is linked to the current value of their property.

Row 5 shows the impact of increases in maintenance and management (M&M) spending since 1979. The rise in M&M spending per dwelling increased the average value of housing benefits in kind by just under £50 per person. Lower income groups have benefited the most from these increases both in absolute *and* proportionate terms. While Right To Buyers are insulated from increases in rents, nor do they benefit from increases in local authority spending on the maintenance and management of their property. Since higher income groups contain more RTB households, it follows that they have benefited less from higher M&M spending. This is offset, to some extent, by the fact that increases in M&M spending per dwelling were greatest for local authority tenants in the top income group (see Figure 4.8).

Row 6 estimates the net impact of the Right To Buy scheme, compared to what would have happened if the scheme had not been introduced (and participants had remained as local authority tenants). According to these estimates, the value of housing benefits in kind is *lower* than if the scheme had not existed (by £9 per person on average). This is because the economic subsidy to RTB households is less than the estimated subsidy they would have received as local authority tenants (see Box 4.1). The impact is lower for the bottom two income groups, which have a smaller proportion of RTB households.

Summary

- Between 1979-93, the overall value of housing benefits in kind was almost unchanged. The amount going to the bottom two income groups increased, while the amount going to higher income groups fell. Thus, the distribution has become more pro-poor over time;

- Since 1979, there has been a significant reduction in the proportion of local authority tenants, only part of which is accounted for by the sale of council properties under the Right To Buy scheme (see Figure 4.2). This explains a large part of the reduction in housing benefits in kind going to the top three quintile groups. The second quintile group was the only one *not* to experience a fall in the proportion of people receiving housing benefits in kind (if we include people living in Right To Buy properties). This partly explains why this income group did better than the bottom income group;

- The other part of the explanation is that local authority tenants in the bottom income group were living in larger households, on average, than in 1979, while the opposite is true of other income groups. This matters because average subsidies per tenant are lower for bigger households;

- Increases in local authority rents had a substantial negative impact on the value of benefits in kind. Tenants in higher income groups experienced the greatest increases in rents, but many of them avoided their impact by exercising the Right To Buy;

- For all except the top income group, the impact of higher rents was more than offset by rising property values and increased spending on the maintenance and management of local authority properties. Thus, the average subsidy per tenant rose significantly in real terms between 1979-93 (see Figure 4.3). Although local authority tenants in higher income groups continue to receive greater subsidies, on average, than those in lower income groups, the differences are smaller than in 1979;

- The net impact of the Right To Buy scheme appears to have been a *reduction* in the value of benefits in kind. This is because those who purchased under the scheme would probably have received a larger economic subsidy if they had remained as local authority tenants (at current rents and property values, etc). The effect may not be as significant as estimated here, but even so, it does *not* support the idea that the Right To Buy was a give-away scheme that favoured better off tenants. The distributional impact of the RTB scheme is relatively small. Lower income groups are least affected, because they contain fewer RTB households.

Chapter Five: Service-by-Service Analysis: Personal Social Services

Background

Public expenditure on the personal social services is summarised in Table 5.1. If we include Income Support to residents of independent residential and nursing homes, net spending increased by around 170 per cent in real terms between 1979-93.[22] This chapter only covers spending on elderly people (aged 65 and over). The increase in spending on this group was greater than the average for all groups. Net expenditure on residential care for the elderly increased five-fold over this period to become by far the largest item of expenditure within the personal social services budget. The amount spent on day and domiciliary care for the elderly has also increased substantially; net spending has more than doubled since 1979.

The biggest modification to policy over this period were the changes to social security regulations in the early 1980s that allowed residents in independent homes to receive means-tested support towards their care costs. (Previously, only residents in local authority homes had been eligible for support.) This initiated a very rapid expansion in the size of the independent home sector - both in absolute terms and relative to the local authority sector. Partly, this was local authorities seeking to shift some of the financial burden of residential care on to central government. But, another reason was the expansion of residential care, and in particular, the nursing home sector, to accommodate those who would formerly have been cared for by the NHS as long-stay patients (see Chapter Three). Responsibility for new residents was transferred back to local authorities in April 1993, since when spending has begun to stabilise. Another important influence on spending was the increase in the size of the elderly population, in particular the very elderly on whom personal social services are heavily concentrated.

---

22   Income Support towards the costs of residential care is not included in conventional measures of cash income, because the beneficiaries are not covered by household surveys. Therefore, this expenditure is allocated as a benefit in kind, even though it is strictly a cash payment.

Table 5.1: Personal Social Services Expenditure in the UK,* 1979-93 (current expenditure, £ million, 1993 prices**)

	1979	1987	1993	% change (1979-93)
Residential care for the elderly				
Net funding from local authorities	648	859	1064	64
Income Support payments by DSS	24	1089	2514	10251
Total	672	1948	3578	432
Non-residential care for the elderly				
Day centres	55	86	142	157
Home helps	423	714	856	102
Meals on wheels	44	57	56	26
Other	61	79	195	218
Total (gross)	584	936	1249	114
Fees and charges	46	85	117	153
Total (net)	538	851	1132	111
Other personal social services*				
Children	859	1178	1438	67
Mentally-ill and learning disabled	222	456	783	253
Younger physically disabled	131	125	157	20
Total	1211	1759	2378	96
Field work and administration***	870	1637	1903	119
Total personal social services				
Net expenditure	3338	6280	9108	173
Fees and charges	128	279	215	68
Gross expenditure	3466	6559	9323	169

*   breakdown of expenditure by service is based on England figures only.
**   expenditure not allocated.
***   adjusted using the Retail Prices Index.
Sources: DoH (1996b)

Methodology

Only expenditure on those aged over 65 is allocated. This accounts for around 60% of all personal social services spending. Expenditure on day and domiciliary care is allocated in a similar way to health care expenditure, using data from the General Household Survey for the nearest year available. The treatment of residential care presents special problems, because the recipients are by definition excluded from household surveys.

The benefits of the residential care support system are allocated to the household population using an insurance-based approach. First, we assign to individuals a probability that they will enter a residential home in that year, based on admissions data for people of their age and gender. This is multiplied by the value of the financial support they would receive if they did enter a home, which in turn depends on their income and capital (as support is means-tested) and their expected length of stay. It is worth noting that the amount of expenditure allocated in this way will not necessarily equal actual expenditure on residential care. One reason is that the incomes of people in the household population may differ from those currently in homes. A more detailed description of the methodology is provided in Appendix 1.

I.   Residential care

Estimates of benefits in kind from residential care are given in Table 5.2 and illustrated in Figure 5.1 below. This shows the very significant increase in the value of this benefit in kind since 1979. The distribution is more pro-poor than for other welfare services, although as for health care, there is a significant hump in the distribution in 1993. Part of the reason for this is that we are only allocating expenditure on those aged over 65, so the distribution is very sensitive to the position of elderly people in the income distribution.

Looking at the distribution of benefits between retired persons (see Figure 5.2), it is not the poorest among the elderly who are benefitting most from residential care support. In 1993, retired persons in the second quintile group receive the greatest value of benefits in kind. So, the hump-shaped distribution for all persons cannot be explained solely by the position of elderly people in the income distribution - although that is clearly a factor, too. The overall distribution is generally less pro-poor than we might expect given that residential care is means-tested. It also becomes less pro-poor over time. The main factors affecting the shape of the distribution are discussed below.

Table 5.2: Benefits in Kind from Residential Care, 1979-93

	1979	1987	1993	Changes: 1979-93 £s	Changes: 1979-93 %
All households					
Bottom	30	52	56	26	87
2	11	57	85	74	673
3	6	22	31	25	417
4	3	8	19	16	533
Top	2	7	8	6	300
All	10	29	49	30	300
Retired households					
Bottom	80	204	267	187	234
2	60	196	298	238	397
3	56	162	201	145	259
4	43	91	185	142	330
Top	35	107	98	63	180
All	67	176	240	155	231

Figure 5.1: Benefits In Kind from Residential Care, 1979-93, All Persons

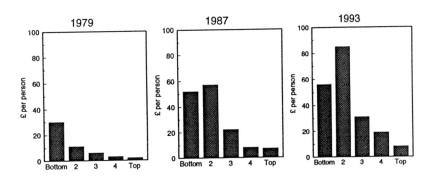

Figure 5.2: Benefits In Kind from Residential Care, 1979-93, Retired Persons

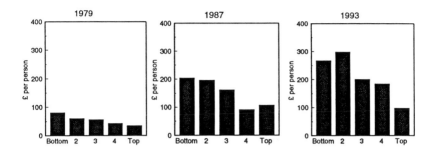

Figure 5.3: Residential Care Support by Age and Gender, 1993

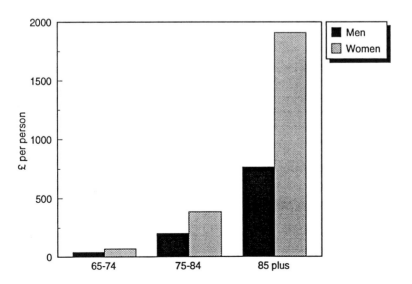

Demographic effects

The need for residential care is closely related to a person's age and gender. In 1993, the probability of being admitted to any home was about 1 in 200 for someone aged 65-74, 1 in 30 for someone aged 65-74, and 1 in 6 for someone over 85. Women were about twice as likely to be admitted as men in the same age group.[23] This is reflected in the distribution of benefits in kind by age and gender (see Figure 5.3).

As a result, changes in the demographic composition of the population will have significant effects on the distribution of benefits in kind from residential care. We focus on the over 75 year olds, since they account for most residential care spending. Figure 5.4 shows that the number of people aged over 75 has increased both as a proportion of the total population and as a proportion of the retired population. The top graph shows that *in the population as a whole*, over 75 year olds have shifted from the bottom income group to higher income groups. This is clearly an important factor in explaining why the distribution of benefits in kind becomes hump-shaped in 1993. However, *within the population of retired persons*, over 75 year olds have become more concentrated towards the bottom of the income distribution. Thus, demographic factors do not explain why the distribution of benefits between retired persons is not as pro-poor as we might expect or why it has become less pro-poor over time.

Admission rates

Between 1979-93 admission rates to all residential homes roughly doubled (see Table 5.3), so that elderly people are now around twice as likely to enter a home than in 1979. Nearly all this increase can be explained by the expansion of the nursing home sector. Since 1979, the number of nursing home places in the United Kingdom has increased from around 25,000 to over 180,000 (Laing and Buisson, 1995). Admission rates to other homes fell slightly in aggregate, but more significant was the shift in the balance of provision from local authority to independent homes. An increase in overall admissions should increase the value of benefits in kind. However, the precise impact depends on the relative cost of different types of home.

---

23   The reasons for this are disputed, but an important factor is that women of a given age are more likely to be single than men and would therefore have less support at home.

Figure 5.4: Distribution of Elderly Population, Aged Over 75

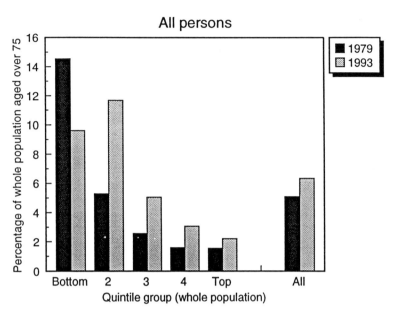

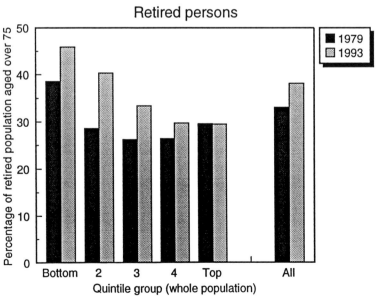

Table 5.3: Admission Rates to Residential Homes, 1979-93

% of household population admitted during year by age group	1979	1987	1993
Local authority homes			
65-74	0.14	0.11	0.05
75-84	0.89	0.60	0.33
85 plus	4.07	3.04	1.58
Independent homes			
65-74	0.03	0.09	0.08
75-84	0.47	0.68	0.70
85 plus	1.77	3.25	3.62
Nursing homes			
65-74	0.05	0.11	0.39
75-84	0.35	0.63	2.29
85 plus	2.30	4.14	10.75
All homes			
65-74	0.22	0.31	0.53
75-84	1.71	1.91	3.32
85 plus	8.13	10.43	15.94

Residential care costs

Residential care fees have risen sharply in real terms. For example, the estimated *gross* cost of supporting a resident in a local authority home has gone up from £75 per week in 1979 to £315 in 1993 (in 1993 prices). For those people already receiving financial support, any increase in the cost of residential care would be met in full by the state. Since the majority of residents are supported, higher fees can be expected to have a significant impact on the value of benefits in kind.

This assumes, of course, that increases in costs reflect an improvement in the standard of service being provided. In practice, at least some of the increase in fees will have been due to the rising costs of provision relative to the general rate of inflation, for the same reasons as the costs of health care have tended to rise in real terms. If possible, purely inflationary increases in costs should be discounted.

There are also significant variations in cost between different types of home. Table 5.4 gives estimates of the gross cost of supporting a 75 year old women over the full duration of her stay. Nursing home costs are low, because average lengths of stay are much shorter than for other homes. This means that the expansion of the nursing home sector will have less impact than we might have expected from looking at admission rates. The difference in the cost of local authority and independent residential homes is also striking. On this basis, the switch between local authority and independent homes will, other things being equal, reduce the value of financial support to residents.

One reason why the cost of local authority homes is so much higher is that residents of local authority homes may be more disabled (and so require more intensive care) than residents of independent homes; this would explain why average lengths of stay (until death) are shorter. A second possible explanation is that additional services are provided to residents of local authority homes, for example chiropody, which are charged extra at other homes. Thirdly, the Department of Social Security imposes limits on the amount it will pay towards the fees of independent and nursing homes, which may not cover the full cost of these homes. In all these cases, the higher cost of care represents a genuine difference in the value of services being provided. A fourth explanation is that local authority homes are simply less efficient than other homes. To the extent that this is the case, the cost differential between local authority and independent homes should not be taken fully reflected in estimates of benefits in kind.

Table 5.4: Typical Gross Cost of Residential Care, 1993

	Local authority home	Independent residential home	Nursing home
Weekly cost (£s)	315	185	280
Average length of stay (months)	27.2	39.8	12.2
Total gross cost (£s)	37,100	31,900	14,800

System of financial support

Unlike most other public services, support for residential care is means-tested. The amount someone is expected to contribute depends on their own income (as opposed to household income) and on the value of their capital. For owner-occupiers who are not living with a partner, this includes the value of their home. For this reason, the amount of support someone receives is not directly related to where they are in the income distribution, which is based on *household* incomes and ignores housing assets.

Table 5.5 shows the amount a 75-84 year old person in each income group would receive if they were admitted to a residential home. These estimates represent the cumulative value of financial support over the expected duration of their stay. The increase in the value of support between 1979-93 is due partly to the extension of support to people in independent and nursing homes and partly to the increase in residential care fees, especially for local authority homes. This is offset by increases in elderly people's income and wealth, in particular the value of their housing equity. Although capital thresholds were relaxed, this does not prevent a decline since 1987 in the average subsidy to people admitted to nursing homes. This also explains why the net cost of support to people in independent homes is only slightly higher in 1993 than in 1987, in spite of the fact that fees went up by over 40 per cent over the same period.

Table 5.5: Net Cost of Residential Care Support, 1979-93 (estimated total cost of supporting a 75-84 year old in residential care over the expected duration of their stay)

Quintile groups	Bottom	2	3	4	Top
Local authority homes					
1979	11,300	10,100	9,400	8,100	5,300
1987	14,200	16,100	11,600	8,000	4,200
1993	21,200	23,800	19,000	14,200	11,300
Independent homes					
1979	-	-	-	-	-
1987	15,300	17,900	11,700	7,800	4,300
1993	16,000	16,800	12,600	8,600	7,200
Nursing homes					
1979	-	-	-	-	-
1987	10,400	10,000	8,900	8,200	6,700
1993	8,300	9,300	7,400	5,200	4,300

Notes: Average for all 75-84 year olds; all figures are in 1993 prices; based on own analysis using Family Expenditure Survey.

The distribution of support between income groups has also changed. In 1979, it was the poorest people entering local authority homes who would be expected to receive the greatest value of support. By 1993, the second quintile group is expected to receive more than the bottom one. The main reason for this is that the bottom income group contains more owner-occupiers than the second and third income groups. As property values have risen during the 1980s, a greater proportion of elderly owner-occupiers at the bottom of the income distribution are no longer eligible for state support towards the costs of residential care (see Figure 5.5).

Figure 5.5: Distribution of Housing Equity, 75-84 year olds

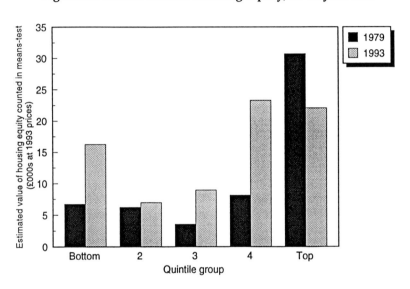

Accounting for distributional changes

The main factors to have affected the distribution of residential care support are:

- the extension of means-tested support to residents of independent residential and nursing homes and subsequent changes to the system of financial support;

- the rapid expansion of the nursing home sector and the switch in the balance of provision from local authority to independent residential homes;

- large increases in residential care fees (in real terms);

- growth in elderly people's incomes and wealth, especially housing equity;
- changes in the demographic composition of the population and of particular income groups;

It is difficult to attribute changes in the distribution of residential care support to individual factors. One problem is that the value of support is affected by changes in people's incomes and wealth. To estimate the impact of demographic changes, we simulate the effects of applying the 1993 system of support to the 1979 population and then compare this to the actual distribution in 1993. However, this will pick up the effects of changes in incomes and wealth, as well as changes in the age and gender composition of the population. A second problem is that there is lot of interaction between the different factors identified above. For example, the impact of extending support to people in residential homes is accentuated by the rise in residential care fees and vice-versa.

With these reservations, Table 5.6 assesses the distributional effects of each of the factors identified above. Box A shows actual changes in value of residential care support between 1979-93. Box B measures the individual effect of each of the changes (in £s per person). Box C presents the same results as in Box B, but as a proportion of total spending in 1993. This is a measure of the proportional impact of the different factors by income group.

As for other services that are concentrated on the elderly, Row 1 shows that changes in the age composition of the population between 1979-93 have led to reduced spending on the bottom income group (by £54 per person on average) and higher spending on other income groups, in particular the second quitile group. For the reasons described above, these figures also capture the effects on the level of financial support received of the growth in people's income and wealth over this period. This would explain why the overall impact of demographic change is close to zero in spite of the fact that the population is ageing. What has happened is that the upward pressure on spending as a result of demographic change has been cancelled out by the effect of people getting richer (and so being eligible for less support).

Row 2 shows that the large increase in admission rates accounts for only a small part of the increase in residential care support since 1979 - around £4 per person on average or 10% of 1993 expenditure. One reason is that much of the expansion took place in the nursing home sector which is cheaper than other types of residential care, because average lengths of stay are so much shorter. The other reason is the switch in residential home admissions from local authority to independent homes, where costs are significantly lower (see Table 5.4).

Table 5.6: Distributional Changes in Residential Care Spending

| | Quintile group | | | | | |
	Bottom	2	3	4	Top	All
A. Distributional changes						+
(£ per person)						
1979	30	11	6	3	2	10
1993	56	85	31	19	8	40
Actual change, 1979-93:						
in real terms	25	74	25	16	6	29
% change	83.5	647.2	453.3	588.2	293.8	281.7
B. Explanatory factors						
(£ per person)						
1. Changes in age composition of population	-54	42	9	0	0	1
2. Changes in admission rates	4	9	3	2	1	4
3. Changes in rules for receiving financial support	41	65	23	15	6	30
4. Increase in residential care fees	21	35	13	8	3	16
C.						
(as a % of 1993 expenditure)						
1. Changes in age composition of population	-97.4	49.7	30.3	46.6	2.5	3.3
2. Changes in admission rates	8.0	10.0	10.3	11.6	10.5	9.6
3. Changes in rules for receiving financial support	73.9	76.2	76.0	77.0	75.9	75.6
4. Increases in residential care fees	38.0	40.6	43.1	43.7	43.9	40.7

Row 3 indicates that the most significant factor contributing to the increase in residential care support was the extension of means-tested support to those in independent homes. Although the bottom two income quintiles benefited the most in absolute terms, the impact was roughly equivalent in proportional terms across income groups (see Box C). As already noted, the impact of extending support to residents of all homes is magnified by increases in residential care fees (see below).

Higher residential care fees (in real term) increased the value of benefits in kind by £30 per person on average (see Row 4). Again, lower income groups benefited more in absolute, but not in proportional terms from these increases. This, of course, assumes that higher fees reflect an improvement in services, which may not be the case.

II.   Non-Residential care

Estimates of benefits in kind from non-residential care are summarised in Table 5.7 and illustrated in Figure 5.6 below. The change in the pattern of benefits in kind is very similar to that for residential care, except that the overall increase in the value of benefits in kind is smaller.

Table 5.7: Benefits In Kind from Non-Residential Care, 1979-93

	1979	1987	1993	Changes: 1979-93	
				£s	%
All households					
Bottom	23	18	22	-1	-4.3
2	13	33	34	21	161.5
3	5	12	14	9	180.0
4	2	5	10	8	400.0
Top	1	2	2	1	100.0
All	9	14	16	7	77.8
Retired households					
Bottom	63	72	107	44	69.8
2	70	113	117	47	67.1
3	48	95	93	45	93.8
4	34	56	96	62	182.4
Top	19	29	32	13	68.4
All	58	85	100	42	72.8

The distribution between retired persons is hump-shaped in all three years (see Figure 5.7). Again, it is slightly surprising that the poorest elderly do not benefit the most, given that there are income-related charges for day and domiciliary services and given that there are more over 75 year olds in the bottom income group (see Figure 5.4).

Figure 5.6: Benefits In Kind from Non-Residential Care, 1979-93 (all persons)

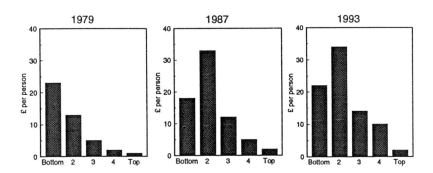

Figure 5.7: Benefits In Kind from Non-Residential Care, 1979-93 (retired persons)

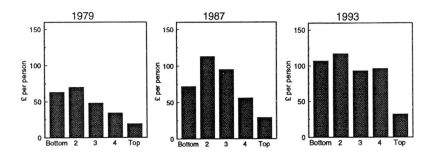

Variations in use of services

To understand the shape of the distribution, it is helpful to examine how the use of these services varies with age, gender, and income group and how significant charges are.

By age and gender

Age and gender are important determinants of the use of non-residential care services (see Figure 5.8), although differences between age groups do not appear to be as large as they are for residential care.[24] Across all age groups, women make greater use of these services than men. However, much of this can be explained by the fact that women are more likely to be single than men of the same age. If we distinguish between single pensioners and pensioner couples, there are still differences between genders, but these are relatively small compared to differences between single people and couples.

Figure 5.9 shows how the balance of spending between age groups has changed between 1979-93. Although all age groups have benefited from an increase in spending, there has been a slight shift in favour of younger age groups. A possible explanation is that there has been an increase in the share of spending on day care, which older age groups use relatively less than domiciliary services.

By income group

The use of day and domiciliary services also varies according to where people are in the income distribution. Income may have a direct influence on the use of services; for example, it determines people's ability to pay for care privately. Alternatively, income may be a proxy for other socio-economic characteristics which affect the need for and demand for these services. Figure 5.10 shows the distribution of spending by income group, after adjusting for differences that are related to age and gender. Other things being equal, it is people in the second quintile group who make the greatest use of non-residential care services. The distribution is similar in both years, although there is some evidence that spending on the bottom two income groups has fallen relative to other income groups.

---

24   Our analysis does not taken into account the intensity of use -only whether someone has made use of a particular service at least once in the last month. If, as seems likely, older people use services more frequently, then our figures will underestimate differences between age groups.

Figure 5.8: Non-Residential Care Spending by Age and Gender, 1993

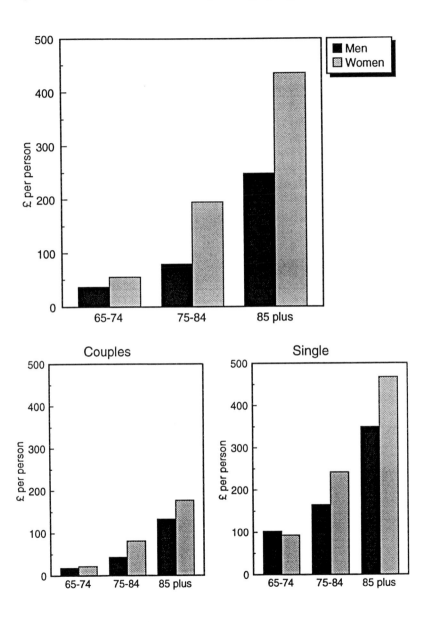

Figure 5.9: Non-Residential Care Spending by Age Group

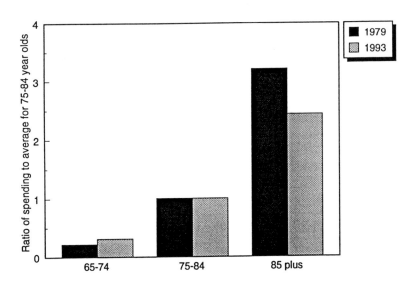

Figure 5.10: Balance of Non-Residential Care Spending by Income Group (after adjustingfor differences related to age and gender)

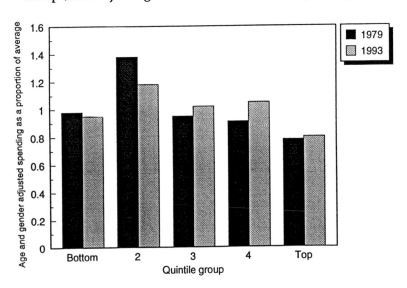

Charges

The overall level of charges has risen slightly since 1979, but revenue is still around 10 per cent of total gross spending (see Table 5.8). It is difficult to determine who bears the brunt of these charges, because they are discretionary and policies vary between local authorities. In this analysis, charges are allocated on a very crude basis to users who are not in receipt of means-tested income support. Thus, an increase in charges will have its greatest impact on higher income groups.

Table 5.8: Charges for Non-Residential Care Services

Charges as a % of gross spending	Home helps	Meals-on-wheels	Day centres	All non-residential care services
1979	5.7	36.4	12.7	9.0
1987	6.6	59.6	5.8	10.0
1993	8.3	69.6	4.9	11.1

Accounting for distributional changes

Table 5.9 analyses changes in the distribution of spending on non-residential care services. The interpretation of the results is the same as for residential care (and other services).

Row 1 shows that changes in the age composition of the population are the most important factor in explaining changes in the distribution of non-residential care spending. The main effects were on the bottom quintile group (a reduction of £14 per person) and the second quintile group (an increase of £16 per person).

An increase in services benefited all income groups, though the effect was small in absolute terms at just £5 per person (see Row 2). Higher income groups benefited more in proportional terms (see Box C), partly because there was a slight shift in spending in favour of the younger elderly; even after adjusting for age and gender effects, there was some shift in favour of higher income groups (see Figure 5.10).

Row 3 shows that higher charges for non-residential services had only a marginal effect. As expected, lower income groups were least affected in proportional terms, because a greater proportion of users in these groups would be exempt from charges.

Table 5.9: Distributional Changes in Non-Residential Care Spending

| | Quintile group | | | | | |
	Bottom	2	3	4	Top	All
A. Distributional changes						+
(£ per person)						
1979	24	13	5	2	1	9
1993	23	35	14	9	2	17
Actual change, 1979-93:						
in real terms	-1	22	9	7	1	8
% change	-3.0	168.7	197.8	328.5	136.9	87.4
B. Explanatory factors						
(£ per person)						
1. Changes in age composition of population	-14	16	6	4	1	3
2. Changes in the use of services	5	7	7	5	1	5
3. Increase in user charges	-0.4	-0.5	-0.6	-0.9	-0.1	-0.5
C.						
(as a % of 1993 expenditure)						
1. Changes in age composition of population	-60.4	44.7	46.0	47.2	39.8	16.1
2. Changes in the use of services	21.7	20.0	50.0	55.6	50.0	29.4
3. Increases in user charges	-1.6	-1.3	-4.3	-10.1	-2.9	-2.9

Summary

Residential care

- Residential care expenditure on the elderly increased over five-fold between 1979-93. Its distribution is more pro-poor than for other welfare services, largely because very elderly people are concentrated towards the bottom of the income distribution. The distribution remains pro-poor throughout the period, though (as for health care) a significant hump appears in the distribution by 1993.

- Demographic factors explain most of the change in the distribution between income groups, but not the overall increase in spending. This is partly because the effect of demographic pressures on spending have been cancelled out by rising incomes and wealth, which will have reduced people's eligibility for means-tested support, other things being equal.

- Whilst admissions have increased significantly, this has been concentrated in the nursing home sector, where average lengths of stay (and hence expenditure per person admitted) are relatively low. Within the residential home sector, there has also been a switch from local authority to independent homes, where care is less expensive. An important question is whether lower costs at independent homes reflect a poorer quality of service or a more efficient one.

- The major factor responsible for higher spending on residential care was the extension of means-tested support to those in independent homes. Also significant was the large increase in residential care fees over this period. Lower income groups benefited more from these changes in absolute terms, but not in proportional terms.

Non-residential care

- Expenditure on non-residential care for the elderly has more than doubled in real terms since 1979. The distribution of these benefits in kind is strongly pro-poor, though it has become less so over the period. Once differences related to age and gender are adjusted for, the distribution is surprisingly flat.

- Non-residential care services are heavily concentrated on very elderly people and particularly on single people within each age group. As for residential care, changes in the age and gender composition of the population account for most of the distributional changes over this period.

- There is some evidence that higher income groups benefited more (in proportional terms) from the increase in spending between 1979-93, though the effects are not large. One reason is that there has been a slight shift in favour of services used by the younger elderly, who are generally better off than the very elderly.

- Higher charges have had only a very small (pro-poor) impact on the distribution of non-residential care expenditure.

Chapter Six: Service-by-Service Analysis: Education

Background

Public expenditure on education increased by just over 20 per cent in real terms between 1979-93 (see Table 6.1). Current spending on schools and further education increased by more than this, but there were cuts in capital and related expenditure (for example school meals). Over this period, there was a decline in the school-age population, so expenditure per pupil increased by more than this. Demographic factors also help to explain why spending on some sectors, for example nursery and primary education, grew faster than others.

While the population of school-age children has fallen, participation rates have gone up. This is because more 3-4 year olds are joining school early and more 16-18 year olds are staying on at school or going on to further education. The number of students in higher education has also risen sharply - by 80 per cent in terms of full-time equivalent students.[25] Most of this expansion has taken place since 1990. However, this has not been reflected in a comparable growth in higher education spending, because funding arrangements have become less generous.

This chapter focuses on the distribution of education spending between different income groups. To what extent can distributional changes be accounted for by purely demographic factors? Who has benefited most from the expansion of nursery education and the increase in the proportion of young people staying on at school and going on to further education? Has higher education become more accessible to all income groups? How have different students been affected by changes to the formula for calculating maintenance payments?

---

25   Part-time students are given a weight of 0.4.

Table 6.1: Education Expenditure in the UK, 1979-93 (current expenditure, £ million, 1993 prices in real terms)

	1979	1987	1993	% change: 1979-93
Schools and further education				
Nursery/primary	5980	6528	8594	44
Secondary	7480	8326	8553	14
Special	885	1113	1403	59
Further education*	2186	2588	3305	51
Total	16531	18555	21855	32
Higher education	5008	5230	5977	19
Related expenditure**	2091	1601	1309	-37
Total education				
Current	23630	25386	29142	23
Capital	1561	1071	1532	-2
Total	25101	26457	30674	22

*   Discretionary awards not allocated (worth around £200m in 1993 or 6 per cent of total spending on further education);

**   Expenditure not allocated.

Methodology

Expenditure on primary, secondary, and special schools is distributed between pupils in each sector, excluding those at independent schools. Subsidies to independent schools in the form of the Assistant Places Scheme[26] and tax relief from charitable status are not taken into account.

Tertiary education is split between further education (which is combined with schools) and higher education. The difficulty in allocating expenditure on higher education is that students living in halls of residence are not covered by household surveys[27] and we know from previous research (Evandrou *et al.*, 1993) that these students are

---

26   Expenditure on the Assisted Places Scheme was £92 million in 1993/4.

27   A further complication is that changes to the system of funding further and higher education make it difficult to produce a consistent time series for expenditure on the different types of institution.

typically from better off families than those who are living at home. Allocating expenditure only to those households with students living at home would underestimate the benefits to higher income groups. To avoid this problem, "non-resident" students are allocated to parental households using UCAS (formerly UCCA) admissions data, which provides a breakdown of acceptances to universities by social class.[28]

Support for tuition fees is distributed only to full-time students, while other recurrent funding is shared between all students (including part-time students) on a full-time equivalent basis. Maintenance payments are calculated using the grant formula, which is based on the parents' or (for mature students) the spouse's income. Some allowance is made for the fact that older students are less likely to be doing their first degree, in which case they would not be eligible for Mandatory Awards.

I. Schools and further education

Estimates of the distribution of benefits in kind from schools and further education are shown in Figure 6.1 below and summarised in Table 6.2. The distribution is hump-shaped in 1979, but becomes more pro-poor over time. The influence of demographic factors is demonstrated by comparing the distribution for all persons with the distribution for non-retired persons only (see Table 6.2). Once elderly people are taken out, changes in the distribution are far less dramatic.

Demographic effects

The distribution of benefits in kind from schools and further education is very sensitive to the position of children in the income distribution. Figure 6.2 shows that there are a greater proportion of school-age children (aged 3-18) in the bottom half of the income distribution,[29] which would explain why the distribution of benefits in kind is essentially pro-poor. However, there were some significant changes between 1979-93. The proportion of school-age children in the bottom income group rose slightly, while the proportion in other income groups fell sharply, particularly in the middle three quintile groups.

---

28 This is done by assigning to household heads aged 42-60 a probability of having a non-resident student based on their social class.
29 The main reason is that children reduce the equivalised income of the household they are living in, because a given income has to be shared out between more people. Another reason is that workers often reach the peak of their earnings capacity after their children have left home.

Overall, the proportion of school-age children (aged 3-18) fell from 25 per cent of the population to 21 per cent. Thus, demographic factors would account, at least in part, for the change from a hump-shaped distribution in 1979 to a more pro-poor distribution in 1993.

Table 6.2: Distribution of School and Further Education Benefits in Kind, 1979-93

	1979	1987	1993	Changes: 1979-93	
				£s	%
All households					
Bottom	320	430	540	220	69
2	420	370	440	20	5
3	380	400	430	50	13
4	300	330	350	50	17
Top	180	220	250	70	39
All	**320**	**350**	**400**	**80**	**25**
Non-retired households					
Bottom	510	570	680	170	33
2	510	520	610	100	20
3	420	470	510	90	21
4	320	360	390	70	22
Top	190	240	270	80	42
All	**380**	**420**	**480**	**100**	**26**

Demographic factors can be controlled for by adjusting expenditure for age. (If the resulting distribution is flat, then the distribution can be attributed to demographic factors alone.) From Figure 6.3, it is clear that demographic factors are responsible for most of the differences between income groups. However, there is a small, but significant, pro-poor slope to the distribution of *age-adjusted* expenditure. The shape of the distribution is similar in both years, but there are some minor changes. For example, the bottom income group does better in 1993 than in 1979, even after controlling for the effects of demographic change. Nor, do demographic factors explain the overall increase in spending on schools and further education. Other things being equal, the fall in the proportion of school-age children would have led to a reduction in total spending.

Figure 6.1: Benefits In Kind from Schools and Further Education, 1979-93

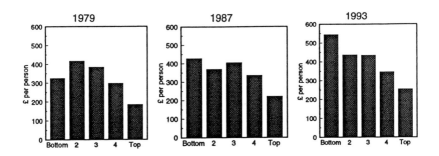

Figure 6.2: Proportion of School-Aged Children by Income Group

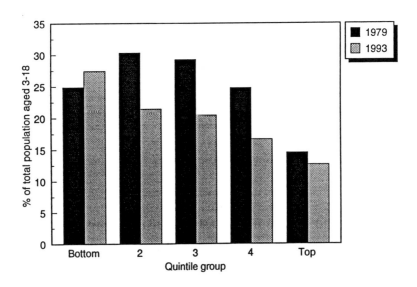

Figure 6.3: Age-Adjusted Spending on Schools and Further Education by Income Group

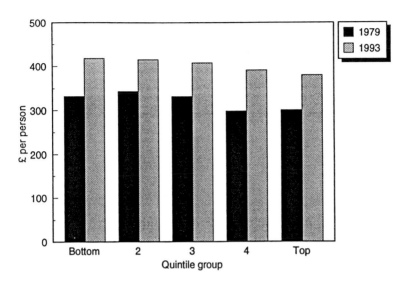

Participation rates

One factor that would explain the pro-poor distribution of age-adjusted expenditure is the differential use of private schools. Since children from higher income groups are more likely to be sent to private schools, participation rates at *state* schools will be higher for children in lower income groups. Figure 6.4 also shows the marked increase in participation rates since 1979, as the proportion of children joining school early and continuing their education beyond 16 has increased over the period. Interestingly, it is higher income groups that have experienced the biggest increases in participation rates.

For mature students (including part-timers), participation rates in further education more than doubled between 1979-93 (see also Figure 6.4). In 1979, the top income group had a higher participation rate than the bottom income group. By 1993, the reverse was true. A possible explanation is that low-wage earners and the unemployed are making greater use of further education as a means of acquiring new skills.

Figure 6.4: Participation Rates in State Schools and Further Education by Income Group

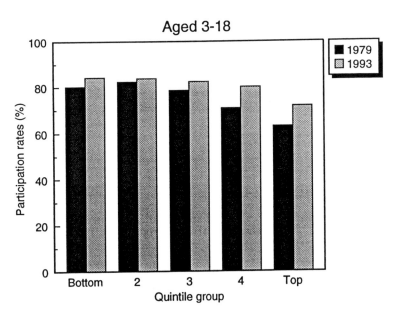

Aged 3-18

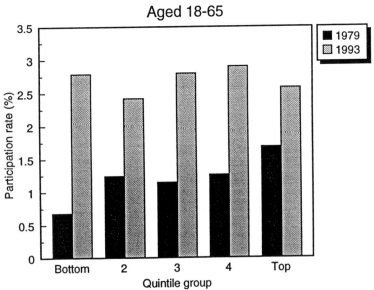

Aged 18-65

Unit costs

Higher participation rates are one reason that expenditure on schools and further education has increased. The other reason is that spending per pupil has gone up, at least in the schools sector. However, the extent to which spending per pupil (or unit costs) has increased depends on how cost inflation is adjusted for. Table 6.3 provides estimates of unit costs in both real and volume terms. Figures in real terms are adjusted using the Retail Price Index, whereas figures in volume terms are adjusted using a special index of salaries and equipment costs in the education sector.

Table 6.3: Unit Costs of Schools and Further Education

£s per full-time equivalent student	1979	1993	% change
Primary:			
Real	1,123	1,723	+53
Volume	1,402	1,723	+23
Secondary:			
Real	1,698	2,516	+48
Volume	2,125	2,516	+18
Special:			
Real	6,557	13,207	+101
Volume	8,185	13,207	+61
Further education (18 and under):			
Real	2,986	3,069	+3
Volume	3,737	3,069	-18
Further education (over 18):			
Real	2,710	2,393	-12
Volume	3,392	2,393	-29

As for other public services, RPI-adjusted figures will probably over-estimate increases in spending, because they ignore the fact that the costs of providing education services have been rising faster than the costs of producing other goods and services in the economy (on which the RPI is based). On the other hand, special price indices ignore productivity improvements and so will under-estimate increases in the value of services. Productivity is particularly hard to measure in the case of education, because there is no standard measure of value added. [30]

Distributional effects arise from differences in unit costs between sectors. For example, unit costs of primary schools are lower than for further education. This will favour higher income groups, because a greater proportion of their benefits in kind are from further education than for lower income groups (see Figure 6.5). However, if we look at *changes* in unit costs over time, schools have done better than further education. Thus, changes in unit costs since 1979 will have benefited lower income groups more than higher income groups.

Figure 6.5: Distribution of Spending on Schools and Further Education, 1993

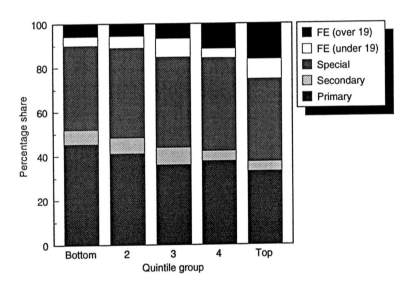

Accounting for distributional changes

The main factors affecting the distribution of benefits in kind from schools and further education are:

---

30 If, for example, exam results are improving, this could mean that pupils are performing better or that the exams are getting easier. Even if it could be shown that pupils' performance has improved, there is no way of knowing if the pupils had more potential to begin with or if it is schools that are more 'productive'. In either case, this assumes that exams are good measure of educational achievement.

- a fall in the proportion of school-age children in the population and a shift in their position in the income distribution;

- an increase in the proportion of children joining school early and staying on beyond 16;

- an increase in the number of mature students in further education, including part-time students;

- changes in unit costs, in particular differences between schools and further education establishments.

The significance of these various factors are examined in Table 6.4. Box A shows what actually happened to the value of benefits in kind going to different income groups. For example, the average amount allocated to people in the bottom income group increased by £220 or 68 per cent between 1979-93. This was a much bigger increase than for other income groups. The second quintile group did least well, experiencing only a 5 per cent increase in the value of benefits in kind. Box B measures the individual effect of the changes identified above on the value of benefits in kind (in £s per person). Box C presents the same figures as a percentage of total spending on each income group in 1993. This shows the proportional effect of changes on different income groups.

Row 1 of Boxes B and C shows how changes in the age composition of the population between 1979 and 1993 have affected the distribution. (This meant more school-age children in the bottom income group and fewer school-age children in other income groups.) The second quintile group received £161 per person less as a result, while the bottom income group received £59 per person more. Thus, demographic changes account for most of the distributional changes over this period. The figure in the last column is a measure of the overall impact of demographic change on spending. Because of changes in the age composition of the population since 1979, spending on schools and further education is an average of £83 per person (or 21 per cent) less than it would otherwise have been. This indicates the extent to which demographic change eased the pressure on education spending. The fact that education spending increased in spite of this is due to increasing participation rates and higher unit costs (see below).

Row 4 measures the effect of higher participation rates. These raised overall spending by £61 per person (or 15 per cent of total spending in 1993). All income groups benefited, but the gains were not distributed evenly between income groups. In absolute terms, the increases were larger for lower income groups (see Box B), but in proportional terms, the increases were larger for higher income groups (see Box C). The latter can be explained by two factors. Firstly, it was the top two income groups that experienced the biggest increases in participation rates for pupils aged under 18 (see Figure 6.4). Secondly, there was a rapid expansion in the size of the further education sector (especially for mature students) relative to other sectors. This also

Table 6.4: Distributional Changes in Spending on Schools and Further Education

	Bottom	2	3	4	Top	All
			Quintile group			
A. Distributional changes						
(£ per person)						
1979	324	416	383	297	184	321
1993	544	436	433	345	253	402
Actual change, 1979-93:						
in real terms	220	20	50	48	69	81
% change	67.9	4.8	13.1	16.2	37.5	25.4
B. Explanatory factors						
(£ per person)						
1. Changes in age composition of population	59	-161	-134	-135	-42	-83
Changes in participation rates:						
2. for those aged 18 and under	50	33	28	42	29	36
3. for those aged over 18	30	19	27	29	17	24
4. Total	79	53	56	71	46	61
Changes in unit costs:						
5. In real terms	171	135	126	94	57	117
6. In volume terms	102	75	38	17	33	53
C.						
(as a % of 1993 expenditure)						
1. Changes in age composition of population	10.9	-37.0	-30.9	-39.3	-16.4	-20.5
Changes in participation rates:						
2. for those aged 18 and under	9.1	7.6	6.6	12.3	11.3	9,1
3. for those aged over 18	5.4	4.4	6.3	8.4	6.7	6.1
4. Total	14.5	12.1	12.8	20.7	18.0	15.1
Changes in unit costs:						
5. In real terms	31.4	31.1	29.0	27.2	22.7	29.0
6. In volume terms	18.7	17.2	8.9	5.0	12.9	13.2

favoured higher income groups, since they receive a greater share of benefits in kind from further education (see Figure 6.5).

Rows 5 and 6 measure the impact of increases in unit costs (or spending per pupil). As for health care, these estimates are sensitive to the price index used for adjusting expenditure in different years. Unit costs increased in both real and volume terms, except in the further education sector, but the increase is smaller if measured in volume terms. On average, the value of benefits in kind is around £117 per person higher if increases in unit costs are measured *real terms* and £53 per person lower if they are measured *in volume terms*. Lower income groups benefited more than higher income groups from the increase in unit costs, both in absolute and proportional terms. For example, spending on the bottom income group was 31 per cent higher than it would have been if unit costs had stayed constant in real terms, whereas the corresponding figure for the top income group is 23 per cent (see Row 5 of Box C). This is because the unit costs of primary, secondary, and special schools increased relative to the unit costs of further education (see Table 6.3). Since lower income groups receive a greater share of benefits in kind from schools compared to higher income groups, these changes in relative unit costs will have favoured lower income groups.

II.   Higher Education

Unlike other welfare services, the distribution of benefits in kind from higher education is pro-rich (see Figure 6.6 and Table 6.5). This is consistent with previous work by Evandrou *et al.* (1993) which produced a similar (pro-rich) distribution using a different data source. The shape of the distribution does not change significantly over the period, except that the bottom income group benefits more than other income groups from the overall increase in spending.

The relatively small increase in the value of benefits in kind is perhaps surprising in view of all the changes that took place over this period. The reason for this is that many of these changes cancelled each other out. While student numbers expanded rapidly in the 1990s, funding per student was cut and maintenance payments became less generous. Each of these changes is explored in turn. Before we do this, though, it is worth considering some of the difficulties in allocating the benefits of higher education subsidies.

Table 6.5: Distribution of Higher Education Benefits in Kind, 1979-93

	1979	1987	1993	Changes: 1979-93 £s	Changes: 1979-93 %
All households					
Bottom	38	75	73	35	92.1
2	68	75	74	6	8.8
3	111	92	118	7	6.3
4	125	103	126	1	0.8
Top	145	148	160	15	10.3
All	97	99	110	13	13.1
Non-retired households					
Bottom	60	97	92	32	53.3
2	81	102	104	23	28.4
3	122	106	138	16	13.1
4	130	112	140	10	7.7
Top	153	158	173	20	13.1
All	113	117	131	20	17.9

Treatment of students

The distribution of benefits in kind from higher education is sensitive to the assumption that students are treated as part of their parents' household. Arguably, benefits in kind should be allocated to students themselves. Since most students have relatively low incomes, the distribution of benefits in kind from higher education would be pro-poor, not pro-rich. However, many students are not financially independent, as this assumption would imply. A significant proportion live at home, while many other students spend time at home during the holidays and so are sharing in their parents' standard of living for at least part of the year. Secondly, the choice to study is an investment towards higher incomes in the future, so, it does not seem very meaningful to treat the beneficiaries as poor. Students may have low incomes as students, but their parents' position in the income distribution is probably more representative of where they themselves will end up in the distribution. Finally, it seems likely that in the absence of government funding, parents of students would bear some, perhaps most, of the cost of educating their children. Thus, parents are also direct beneficiaries of higher education subsidies.

Although there is no right or wrong way of handling students, the methodology used here has the advantage of being consistent over time and consistent between students.[31] Attaching students to parental households also enables us to incorporate non-resident students who would otherwise be missing from household surveys. (University admissions data includes information on the socio-economic class of applicants' parents and so provides a ready way of doing this.) Furthermore, the link between students and their parents allows us to calculate maintenance payments, which are based on parental incomes.

Figure 6.6: Benefits In Kind from Higher Education, 1979-93

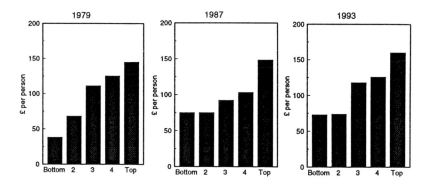

Demographic effects

The majority of higher education spending is directed at 18-24 year olds. The distribution of benefits in kind from higher education is, therefore,

---

31   If we attempted to allocate the benefits to students, it would be difficult to know how to treat students who were living at home. Should we split them from the rest of the household and position them in the income distribution on the basis of their personal income, even though they are sharing their parents' house (and probably more besides)? Or should we treat them as part of their parents' household (and therefore differently from other students), even though they may only be at home because their household was interviewed during the holidays? Either way, there would be inconsistencies in the way different students were treated.

affected by the position of 18-24 year olds in the income distribution. Figures 6.7 shows that this age group are concentrated towards the upper end of the income distribution. In 1979, almost 15 per cent of the top income group was made up of 18-24 year olds, compared to just 5 per cent of the bottom income group. This is obviously an important factor in explaining the pro-rich distribution of benefits in kind.

Figure 6.7: Distribution of 18-24 Year Olds by Income Group

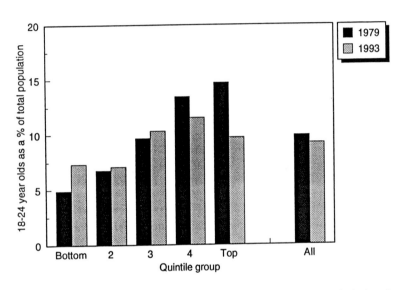

Between 1979 and 1993, there was a significant shift in the distribution of 18-24 year olds within the income distribution. Although there are still more 18-24 year olds in higher income groups, the differences are less marked than in 1979. Other things being equal, this should have produced a more equal distribution of benefits in kind. Overall, there was a small, but significant, reduction in the proportion of 18-24 year olds in the population. This will have reduced pressures on higher education spending.

Participation rates

Admissions data show that children of parents from higher socio-economic groups are more likely to enter higher education. Since expenditure is allocated to parents, we would expect the proportion of 18-24 year olds in higher education (or the 'participation rate') to increase as we move up the income distribution. As Figure 6.8 shows, participation rates are indeed higher for richer income groups.

But, more significantly, differences between the top and bottom income groups are now much greater than in 1979. What this appears to show is that it is higher income groups who have benefited most from the expansion of higher education (although accessibility has improved for all income groups).

The story for mature students is very different (see also Figure 6.8). In 1979, the middle income group made the greatest use of higher education and the top and bottom ones very little. By 1993, all income groups were making roughly equal use of higher education. Since mature students are assessed on their own income (and not their parents' income), full-time mature students are unlikely to be very high in the income distribution unless they have a rich partner. The increased use by higher income groups may be due to the increased availability of part-time courses, which can be combined with full-time work.

Unit costs

Table 6.6 shows how sharp the cuts in spending per student have been since 1979. In real terms, unit costs are lower by 30-40 per cent. Part of the explanation is that ex-polytechnics have expanded faster than older universities, and the former have always had lower unit costs. (This would have brought the average down even if average spending within each sector had not changed.) But, there have also been cuts in spending within institutions, as they have been encouraged to take on more students with less than proportionate increases in funding. Lower unit costs should be reflected in a lower value of benefits in kind, unless it can be shown that there have been genuine efficiency gains. For example, if there was spare capacity in universities, some increase in student numbers could have been achieved at little additional cost.

Table 6.6: Unit Costs Of Higher Education

£s per full-time equivalent student, 1993 prices	1979	1993	% change
Higher education (18-24):			
Real	7,266	5,068	-30
Volume	9,095	5,068	-44
Higher education (25 plus):			
Real	6,557	4,013	-39
Volume	8,208	4,013	-51

Figure 6.8: Participation Rates in Higher Education by Income Group

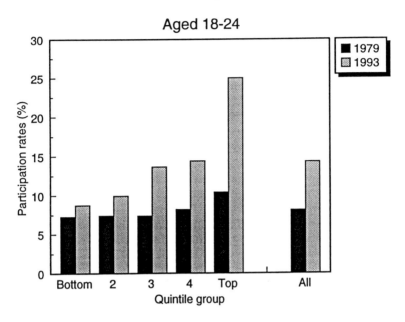

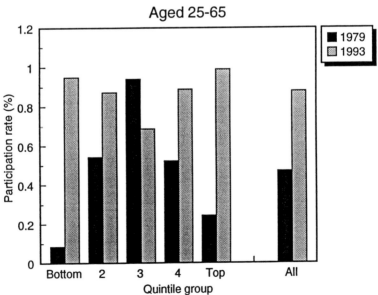

Falling unit costs will hit higher income groups more than lower income groups - in both absolute and proportionate terms. This is because students from lower income groups receive a greater share of their subsidy in the form of maintenance payments and a smaller share through the funding of higher education institutions, which is what is being measured here (see Figure 6.9).

A significant change to the system of funding over this period was the reduction in the share of government subsidies in the form of block grants to universities - from 84 per cent in 1979 to 63 per cent in 1993 - and a corresponding increase in the share paid in tuition fees (through Mandatory Awards). The main aim was to encourage an increase in higher education places by linking funding more closely to student numbers. The other effect was to target subsidies at first-time undergraduates, as opposed to post-graduates or part-time students. As block grants were reduced, universities were forced to raise their tuition fees, but only the tuition fees of first-time undergraduates are automatically paid by local education authorities. This explains why the cuts in unit costs were greater for mature students, since they are less likely to be doing their first degree and more likely to be studying part-time. The distributional effects work against lower income groups, because a greater proportion of the subsidies they receive go to mature students than for higher income groups (see Figure 6.10). However, this effect is unlikely to be very significant.

Maintenance payments

Maintenance payments are part of the Mandatory Awards that are made to all full-time students doing their first degree. The amount received is means-tested using a formula that is amended each year. Since 1979, the maximum value of the grant has been reduced in real terms and changes have been made to the method of calculating the parental contribution. As a result, the average value of maintenance payments has fallen and payments are now more closely targeted at students from less well-off households (see Figure 6.11). The reason that maintenance payments have fallen more sharply for students in higher quintile groups is partly because the average income of these quintile groups has risen faster and partly because the schedule for parental contributions is now steeper than before.

As the proportion of mature and part-time students has increased, a greater number of students do not qualify for any maintenance payments. If we include these students, the average value of maintenance payments will have fallen by even more than shown in Figure 6.11.

Figure 6.9: Composition of Higher Education Subsidies by Income Group, 1993

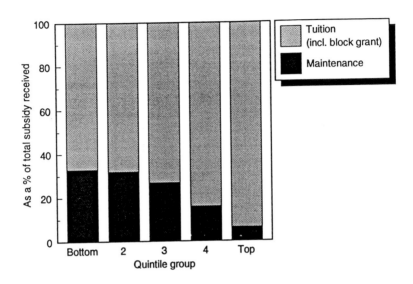

Figure 6.10: Spending on Mature Students by Income Group, 1993

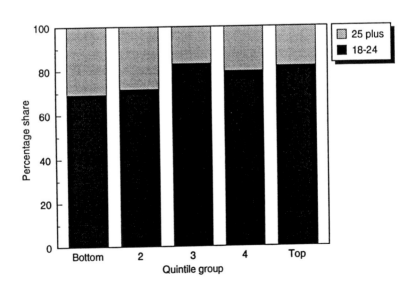

Figure 6.11: Value of Maintenance Payments by Income Group, 1979-93

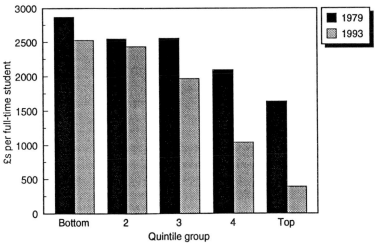

Source: Own calculations using FES.

Accounting for distributional changes

The main factors responsible for changes in the distribution of benefits in kind from higher education are:

- changes in the demographic composition of the population, in particular the position of 18-24 year olds in the income distribution.

- improved accessibility to higher education for both non-mature and mature students.

- cuts in the amount of funding per student by between 30-40 per cent in real terms since 1979.

- reductions in the maximum value of maintenance payments (in real terms) and changes to the formula for calculating parental or spouse's contributions.

Table 6.7 examines the distributional impact of these changes. Box A shows how the distribution of benefits in kind actually changed between 1979-93. Boxes B and C show the individual impact (by income group) of the various changes identified above.

Row 1 measures the effect of demographic changes. For example, changes in the distribution of the student-age population led to higher spending on the bottom income group (worth £17 per person) and lower

113

spending on the top income group (worth £66 per person). This is one reason why the bottom income group experienced a larger increase in benefits in kind than higher income groups. Overall, demographic changes reduced spending by £15 per person because of a falling proportion of 18-24 year olds in the population. This is a measure of the extent to which the reduction in the student-age population reduced pressure on higher education spending.

Rows 2 and 3 measure the distributional effects of changing participation rates. Row 3 shows clearly that it was higher income groups that benefited most from the expansion in the number of *non-mature* students (see Figure 6.8). For example, spending on the top income group was higher by £77 per person as a result of increases in the participation rate of 18-24 year olds in that income group. For the bottom income group, the corresponding figure is just £8 per person. This increase was also worth proportionally more to the top income group (48 per cent as compared to 11 per cent for the bottom income group).

In the case of mature students (Row 3), the benefits of higher participation rates were greatest at the extremes of the income distribution. In proportional terms, this was worth more to the bottom income group, because a greater proportion of higher education students in the bottom income group are mature students (see Figure 6.10). Row 4 is the sum of Rows 2 and 3.

Rows 5 and 6 measure the effects of reduced funding per student. Row 5 shows how much lower higher spending is as a result of cutting unit costs in real terms. Row 6 does the same, but with unit costs measured in volume terms, which suggests the cuts were even bigger. Lower unit costs reduced overall spending on higher education by between £40-70 per person, depending on which price index is used. Higher income groups were the worst affected in proportional (as well as absolute) terms. This is because students in lower income groups receive a greater proportion of their subsidy in the form of maintenance payments and a smaller share through the funding of higher education institutions, which is what is being measured here.

Row 7 estimates the impact of cutting maintenance payments. As expected, higher income groups were worst affected. The average value of benefits in kind received by people in the top income group was £33 per person (or around 20 per cent) lower than if the value of maintenance payments had been kept at 1979 levels (in real terms). This is very significant, even in relation to the other major changes that occurred during this period. Lower income groups were also affected by the reduction in maintenance payments, but to a much lesser extent.

Table 6.7: Distributional Changes in Higher Education Spending

	Quintile group					
	Bottom	2	3	4	Top	All
A. Distributional changes						
(£ per person)						
1979	38	68	111	125	145	97
1993	73	74	118	126	160	110
Actual change, 1979-93:						
in real terms	35	6	7	1	15	13
% change	92.1	8.8	6.3	0.8	10.3	13.1
B. Explanatory factors						
(£ per person)						
1. Changes in age composition of population	17	-3	-7	-16	-66	-15
Changes in participation rates:						
2. for those aged 18 and under	8	14	45	44	77	38
3. for those aged over 18	21	8	-7	11	22	11
4. Total	29	22	38	55	99	49
Changes in unit costs:						
5. In real terms	-23	-24	-39	-50	-72	-42
6. In volume terms	-41	-42	-71	-89	-128	-74
7. Changes in level of maintenance payments	-3	-1	-9	-20	-33	-13
C.						
(as a % of 1993 expenditure)						
1. Changes in age composition of population	23.3	-4.1	-5.9	-12.7	-41.3	-13.6
Changes in participation rates:						
2. for those aged 18 and under	11.4	18.9	38.1	34.9	48.1	34.2
3. for those aged over 18	28.8	10.6	-5.6	8.4	13.8	9.9
4. Total	40.2	29.5	32.5	43.3	61.9	44.1
Changes in unit costs:						
5. In real terms	-31.5	-32.4	-33.1	-39.7	-45.0	-37.7
6. In volume terms	-56.2	-56.8	-60.2	-70.6	-80.0	-67.3
7. Changes in level of maintenance payments	-4.5	-1.5	-8.0	-16.2	-20.7	-12.2

Summary

Schools and further education

- The distribution of benefits in kind from schools and further education is hump-shaped in 1979, but has become more pro-poor over time (see Figure 6.1). Demographic factors are largely responsible for the shape of the distribution, since this is very sensitive to the position of school-age children in the income distribution. However, there is an underlying bias in favour of lower income groups, because higher income groups make greater use of private education;

- Between 1979-93, the average value of benefits in kind increased by over 30 per cent (see Table 6.2). This happened in spite of a significant reduction in the size of the school-age population. Higher participation rates and greater spending per pupil were responsible for the overall increase in spending (see below);

- Changes in the distribution of benefits were mostly accounted for by demographic factors, in particular an increase in the proportion of school-age children in the bottom income group and a reduction in the proportion of school-age children in other income groups (see Figure 6.2);

- All income groups benefited from increases in participation rates under and over the compulsory schooling age. Higher income groups benefited more in proportional terms, partly because they experienced the biggest increases in participation rates for pupils aged under 18 (see Figure 6.4);

- Spending per pupil (or unit costs) went up over this period, although the increase was smaller when measured in volume terms. Increases were highest in the school sector and lowest in the further education sector (see Table 6.3). This favoured lower income groups who receive a greater proportion of their benefits from spending on schools and a smaller proportion from further education (see Figure 6.5).

Higher education

- The distribution of benefits from higher education are pro-rich. This is partly because there are more student-age children living in well-off households, and partly because children from well-off households are more likely to enter higher education;

- The average value of benefits in kind increased by around 14 per cent over the period. The bottom income group benefited more than other income groups, although the distribution is still heavily skewed in favour of higher income groups (see Figure 6.6);

- Changes in the age composition of the population reduced higher education spending on the top two income groups and increased spending on the bottom income group (see Figure 6.7). Thus, in the absence of demographic change, the distribution would have been more pro-rich in 1993;

- Higher income groups benefited most from the expansion in the number of *non-mature* students (aged 18-24), accentuating differences in participation rates between income groups (see Figure 6.8). Participation rates for *mature* students are fairly even between income groups. Increases since 1979 have benefited the top and the bottom income groups most;

- Lower funding per student (or unit costs) explains why total spending has not increased in line with the expansion in student numbers (see Table 6.6). This affected all income groups, but the impact was greater in proportionate terms for higher income groups. This is because funding to universities forms a greater proportion of the total subsidy they receive. The other subsidy is in the form of maintenance payments, which are worth more to lower income groups (see Figure 6.9).

- The effects of reduced maintenance payments were quite severe, especially for the top two income groups (see Figure 6.11). In both cases, the value of benefits in kind from higher education would have been around one fifth higher if the value of maintenance payments had been kept at their 1979 levels (in real terms).

Chapter Seven: Local Variations

Background

Thus far, little attention has been paid to local variations in spending on welfare services, either at a regional or sub-regional level. By local variations, we mean differences in spending that are related purely to the region (or sub-region) in which a person or household lives, as opposed to other characteristics. To the extent that the use of services varies between regions because of differences in the age, gender, or social class of its residents, this will already be taken into account. For example, Northern Ireland is allocated a greater spending per person on education than other regions, because it has a younger population. What is not captured, though, is that some regions spend more per pupil than other regions or that the cost of an in-patient stay may be higher in some areas than others. Nor are sub-regional variations in spending taken into account. These may be very significant, particularly where funding mechanisms are designed to target resources to areas of greater need.

Local variations are of interest in themselves. However, in this report, we are specifically concerned with their distributional implications. Some regions, in particular Greater London, have a disproportionate share of their population in the top half of the income distribution, while residents of other regions, for example the West Midlands, are concentrated towards the bottom end of the distribution (see Figure 7.1). Similarly, within regions, some areas (e.g. Merseyside) will be poorer than others (e.g. Cheshire). Clearly, local variations in spending could have an effect on the distribution of benefits in kind.

Some difficulties

Unfortunately, there are a number of difficulties in exploring local variations in benefits in kind. The first set of problems are practical, largely to do with the limitations of the data. A particular problem is that, for reasons of confidentiality, household surveys only identify the region in which respondents live, and not the local authority or other, more localised, areas. Thus, it is impossible to take direct account of *sub-regional* variations in the use of welfare services. This is likely to be more of an issue for those services where there is a high degree of local autonomy in spending decisions, such as education. Housing is an even more extreme case, where living one or two streets apart can make all the difference to the value of council housing, even for otherwise similar properties.

Figure 7.1: Distribution of Regional Populations by Income Group, 1993

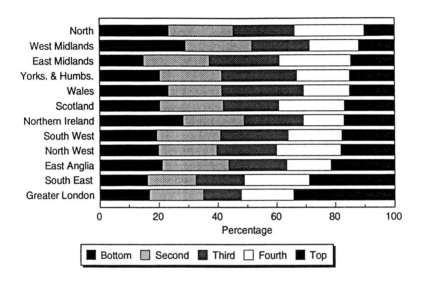

A further problem in using household surveys to examine local variations is that the sample is not designed for carrying out regional analysis, let alone sub-regional analysis. Although the sampling frame draws on households from all regions, the principal focus is to ensure that surveys are representative of different family types. What this means is that if, say, 25 per cent of single pensioners in the survey were in the bottom quintile group, then it would be reasonable to assume that the same held true for the population of single pensioners as a whole (subject to small and known margins of error). However, if 25 per cent of households interviewed from the North were in the bottom quintile group, we could not *necessarily* assume that this held true for the population of Northerners as a whole. There is, however, little that can be done about this other than to recognise that regional figures will be subject to larger, and unknown, margins of error.[32]

---

32 Larger samples would be needed to ensure that household surveys were representative of the regional composition of the population, as well as the composition of family types.

The second set of problems are methodological, which have to do with the proper interpretation of local variations in spending (assuming these can be identified). As noted in Chapter One, a key assumption of this kind of analysis is that the amount spent on a particular service is a good measure of the benefits provided to users of that service. It follows from this assumption that differences in spending between regions should be measuring differences in the intensity or quality of services being provided. But, this may not be the case. For example, an NHS in-patient stay could be more expensive in some regions, because a more skilled surgeon is used or because more after-care is provided. In this case, the extra cost reflects a genuinely better service, which should be taken into account in estimates of benefits in kind. However, higher costs might equally be due to a less efficient use of resources or more expensive inputs. In that case, the difference in spending between regions would not be capturing differences in the value of services, which is what we really want to measure.

Ideally, we would like to distinguish differences in spending that reflect differences in efficiency from differences that reflect the type of service being provided. If we assume that unit costs are the same in all regions, then we are effectively assuming that the service being provided is the same in all regions and that any differences in actual unit costs are due to differences in efficiency between regions. If, on the other hand, we use actual unit costs (by region) to measure benefits in kind, then we are assuming that differences in unit costs solely reflect differences in the intensity or quality of the service being provided and that efficiency is the same in all regions. The report, so far, has been based on the first of these assumptions (i.e. uniform unit costs). In the next section, we explore the distributional impact of applying the second assumption (i.e. actual unit costs). In practice, both assumptions are extreme and the truth is likely to lie somewhere between the two.

In the final section, we take a look at ways in which the system of funding different welfare services steers greater resources to some areas than others and consider the potential distributional impact of these *sub-regional* variations in spending.

I.   *Regional variations*

This section examines the distributional impact of regional variations in spending The analysis is only carried out for 1993 and only for two major services, schools and hospital and community health services. For practical reasons, the analysis is also restricted to Great Britain .[33] The

120

aim is to get a feel for the potential margin of error from ignoring these variations in our earlier analysis.

Schools

In Chapter Six, expenditure on primary schools was distributed evenly between all primary-school children in the United Kingdom, and similarly for children in secondary and special schools. But this ignores regional variations in spending per pupil (or unit costs). For example, spending in Greater London is, on average significantly higher than in other regions, particularly Wales.

Table 7.1: Differences in Unit Costs of Schools by Region, 1993

Standard region	Average unit cost per pupil* (£s)	School benefits in kind per capita (unadjusted)	School benefits in kind per capita (adjusted for unit cost differences)
North	1,810	317	297
Yorks and Humbs.	1,829	293	280
North West	1,806	317	301
East Midlands	1,860	367	360
West Midlands	1,823	367	350
East Anglia	1,819	333	317
Greater London	2,149	285	323
South East	1,838	390	296
South West	1,789	308	287
Wales	1,824	340	329
Scotland**	2,386	376	462
All	**1,911**	**324**	**324**

*   Excluding special schools.
**   Estimated from average unit costs that include special schools.
Source: Handbook of Education Unit Costs, Scottish Rating Review, own calculations using Family Expenditure Survey.

---

33   The reason for this is that the calculation of health care unit costs relies on accurate estimates of the use of services by region. These are based on data from the General Household Survey, which only covers Great Britain. Thus, for the purposes of this analysis, Northern Ireland is excluded.

Table 7.1 shows the average value of school benefits in kind by region, before and after regional variations in spending per pupil have been taken into account. For most regions, the differences are quite small, except for Greater London and Scotland. Variations *within* regions are much more significant (see below). The distribution between income groups is almost unaffected (see Table 7.2). Greater benefits in kind are allocated to Greater London, which will tend to have a pro-rich impact, but this is offset by the pro-poor impact of allocating more to Scotland.

Table 7.2: Impact of Unit Cost Differences on Schools Spending by Income Group, 1993

Income group	Unadjusted figures	Adjusted for unit cost	Difference
Bottom	452	451	-1
2	366	366	0
3	355	352	-3
4	281	283	+2
Top	172	173	+1

Hospital and Community Health Services

In Chapter Three, we allowed for variations in the *use* of health care services between regions, but we did not we allow for regional variations in the unit cost of providing these services (i.e. the cost per treatment). The assumption is that an in-patient stay is an in-patient stay and costs the same wherever you are in the country. In practice, the mix of treatments varies between regions and some forms of treatment are more expensive to perform than others. Even the same treatment may cost significantly more in some areas than others.

Regional variations in health care spending arise largely from historical precedent. Traditionally, spending per capita has been higher in Greater London than elsewhere, because the capital has a disproportionate number of hospitals. This was the issue addressed by the Resource Areas Working Party (RAWP) in the 1970s, which sought to redirect funding to where need was greatest, rather than to where hospitals were currently located. Since then, disparities between regions have been reduced, but funds are still not allocated solely on the basis of needs-related criteria.

Table 7.3: Unit Cost by Region for NHS Hospital and Community Health Services, 1993

Standard region	Share of total spending (%)	Share of allocated benefits (%)	Measure of relative unit costs
North	5.45	6.02	0.91
Yorks and Humbs.	8.20	11.12	0.74
North West	11.49	10.36	1.11
East Midlands	6.53	6.52	1.00
West Midlands	8.45	8.43	1.00
East Anglia	3.20	3.60	0.89
South East (incl. Greater London)	32.39	29.61	1.09
South West	7.62	8.83	0.86
Wales	4.94	5.45	0.91
Scotland	11.74	10.06	1.17

Source: DoH (1995a); own calculations using GHS and FES.

The first column of Table 7.3 shows the regional distribution of NHS spending on Hospital and Community Health Services (HCHS), based on actual expenditure figures for the fourteen Regional Health Authorities.[34] The figures in the second column are the shares of HCHS benefits in kind allocated to each region, as calculated in Chapter Three of this report. The latter were based on differences in the *use* of health care services, but did not take into account regional variations in *unit costs*. The figures in the first column use actual expenditure data and so incorporate variations in unit costs, as well as variations in the use of services by region. The ratio between the first two columns is, therefore, a measure of relative unit costs between regions. For example, actual spending figures for Greater London show that over 32 per cent of total HCHS spending was in the South East, yet in our previous analysis (which assumed uniform unit costs) the share allocated to this region was only 29.6 per cent. The inference is that this difference is accounted for by unit costs being higher in the South East than average (by around 10 per cent.)

---

34   Official NHS spending figures are provided for Regional Health Authorities, whose boundaries are slightly different to those of the Standard Regions referred to throughout this analysis. Where the two do not coincide, spending is allocated between Standard Regions on a simple capita basis.

From the third column of Table 7.3, unit costs appear to be higher-than-average in the South East (including Greater London), the North West, and Scotland, average in the Midlands, and lower-than-average in other regions. The range in unit costs is very significant - from 25 per cent below the average in Yorkshire and Humberside to almost 20 per cent above the average in Scotland.

Figure 7.4 shows the impact on the distribution of benefits in kind of making an adjustment for regional differences in unit costs (using the figures calculated in Table 7.3). The effect is a slight, but definite, shift in favour of higher income groups. The reason for this is that those regions with higher-than-average unit costs are over-represented in the top half of the income distribution and vice-versa.

Table 7.4: Impact of Unit Cost Differences on Spending on Hospital Services by Income Group, 1993

Income group	Unadjusted figures	Adjusted for unit cost	Difference
Bottom	405	403	-2
2	491	488	-3
3	408	401	-7
4	335	340	+5
Top	307	314	+7

II.   Sub-regional variations

Even within regions, there can be significant variations in spending between local authorities or even schools or hospitals within the same area. In part, these result from the exercise of local autonomy in spending decisions. Increasingly, though, differences are reflected in the funding formulae used to distribute public expenditure to and within regional and local bodies. These formulae are designed to ensure an equitable distribution of resources between areas and include various factors aimed at targeting government support to people with greater needs (or at least the areas where they live).

In some cases, current funding arrangements are relatively new and so may not have been operating during the period covered by our analysis. Nevertheless, it is worth considering the implications that the current system might have had for the distribution of benefits in kind between income groups. To begin with at least, new systems of funding often mimic the distribution of resources under the old system, so that looking at what is happening now should give us a fair idea as to what was happening in 1993 (the end of our period). The advantage of looking at funding formulae is that they are more transparent than the more discretionary systems of funding they replaced. This rests on the assumption that allocated funding is a reasonably accurate guide to actual spending. The greater the discretion exercised by spending bodies, the more tenuous this assumption becomes.

The objective of this analysis is to identify variations in spending that have not been captured in our preceding analysis and, where possible, to gauge the likely distributional impact of these variations.

Schools

Funding for nursery, primary, and special schools is distributed to local authorities through block grants (known as Standard Spending Assessments) which cover education and other local authority services. The education component of SSAs is calculated using a formula, which allocates around three quarters of the total budget on the basis of pupil numbers and resident population. The other main element, which makes up around 20 per cent of the total, is for "additional education needs" to compensate for the extra cost of educating children from poorer social backgrounds. The allowance for additional education needs generates significant differences in the amount of government support per pupil between Local Education Authorities. This is reflected in large differences in actual spending per pupil between LEAs (see Figure 7.2).

LEAs are in turn required to distribute at least 85 per cent of their budget to schools using an objective formula. These formulae vary between LEAs. Again, the majority of funding must be allocated on the basis of pupil numbers (weighted for age), but other factors may include indicators of social need. Thus, mechanisms exist for channelling extra funds to schools in less well-off areas, much of which must be assumed to benefit children from poorer households.

The distributional impact of targeted funding is estimated here on the bold assumption that 80 per cent of schools funding is equally distributed to all pupils, but that the remaining 20 per cent (i.e. the share accounted for by the additional education needs allowance) is distributed only to those pupils who are receiving free school meals. (The number of children receiving free school meals is one of the indicators of social need used by many LEAs in their funding formulae). This is obviously an extreme assumption, since some LEAs may not target all the additional funding they receive to schools in the most deprived areas and, in any case, the benefits will be shared by other (better-off) children who are attending schools in those areas. Nevertheless, Table 7.5 shows that the *potential* distributional effects of needs-related variations in funding for schools could be very significant, benefiting the bottom income group at the expense of the top three quintile groups.

Figure 7.2: Impact of Unit Cost Differences on Schools Spending by Income Group, 1993

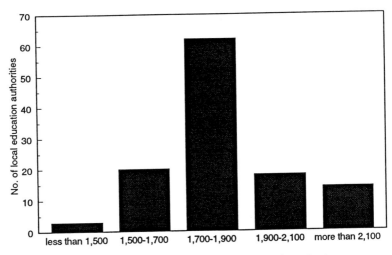

Unit cost of nursery, primary, and secondary schools

Table 7.5: Potential Impact of Needs-Related Variations in Spending on Schools, 1993

Income group	Unadjusted figures	Adjusted for needs-related funding	Difference
Bottom	490	632	+142
2	388	395	+7
3	367	312	-55
4	291	234	-57
Top	189	151	-38

Further and higher education

Funding for further and higher education is distributed directly to institutions by the Further Education Funding Council (FEFC) and the Higher Education Funding Council (HEFC). The funding formulae used by the FEFC and the HEFC are based on student numbers, the mix of courses, and various performance measures. Neither formula takes account of the socio-economic conditions in the areas in which the institutions are based, so there is no mechanism for directing funding towards poorer areas.[35]

This does not mean that there are not large variations in funding levels between institutions, especially in the higher education sector. In 1994/5, the average unit cost per undergraduate student ranged from £2,850 at the University of Luton to £6,970 at the University of Oxford. In general, older universities have significantly higher unit costs than former polytechnics, although the differential is being reduced. This is likely to favour higher income groups, since admissions data (before the two types of institution were combined) show that students going to older universities came from higher socio-economic groups, on average, than students going to ex-polytechnics.

Health care

Revenue allocations for Hospitals and Community Health Services (HCHS) are now made direct to integrated Health Authorities (HAs) using a weighted capitation formula. The new formula for HAs is based on the size of the resident population weighted for the age structure of the population, needs indices, and a market forces factor (which allows for differences in the costs of providing services between areas). The needs indices - one for acute services and one for psychiatric services - contain a mix of socio-economic variables (e.g. the proportion of unemployed, the proportion of pensionable age living alone) and health indicators (e.g. Standardised Mortality Ratios), which are designed to measure relative health needs between areas. Health Authorities (HAs) then buy health care services from hospitals, so the distribution of spending between patients will depend on how their priorities are reflected in their purchasing decisions. For GP fundholders, the aim is to move towards similar capitation-based formulae for budget-setting

---

35 The FEFC does make allowance for the fact that fees are not charged to people in receipt of unemployment benefit or means-tested benefits, but this is already taken into account in our estimates.

(incorporating local needs indicators), although there will be some flexibility in the system at a local level.

Our own estimates of the use of health care services are based on a regression analysis of demographic and socio-economic variables, which include some of the same factors included in the formulae used to allocate funding to HAs. Our equations do not include health indicators but the effects should be picked up, if only in part, by other variables. Thus, even sub-regional variations in spending will be reflected in our distribution, at least to some extent.

The implication of not fully capturing the variations in spending is that our estimated distribution of health care is probably not as pro-poor as it should be. This is because mortality rates, which are taken into account in funding formulae but not in our estimates, are generally higher in poorer areas. The extent of this bias is hard to gauge. Among other things, it depends on the purchasing decisions of HAs and, in particular, the extent to which the additional resources received in areas with higher mortality rates are actually directed at poorer patients.

Personal Social Services

Funding for personal social services, like the schools budget, is allocated through Standard Spending Assessments (SSAs). The elderly PSS block consists of separate assessments of the number of elderly people potentially in need of either residential or non-residential care. Factors taken into account include the incidence of long term limiting illness and the proportion of elderly people living alone. In addition, greater weight is given in the formula for residential care to those aged over 75 and 85. In practice, local authorities have a significant amount of flexibility in setting their own budgets. It is, therefore, unlikely that all the observed variation in services between authorities can be accounted for by differences in funding allocations.

In the case of *non-residential* care, our analysis takes into account variations in the use of services that are related to socio-economic characteristics and income, but not indicators of ill-health. As for health care, our estimates should have captured some of the variation in spending between areas. To the extent that we have not captured needs-based factors, our estimates are likely to understate how pro-poor the actual distribution is.

In the case of *residential* care, the probability of being admitted to a home was based on age and gender only, and so does not vary by region or sub-region except in so far as the age/sex structure of the populations are different. In practice, admission rates to local authority

128

homes vary widely between authorities, even within age groups. Admission rates are particularly low in Greater London authorities (12-13 per 1,000 population aged 75 and over, compared to 19 for England as a whole). On the other hand, unit costs (which we also assume to be the same everywhere) are significantly higher in London authorities than in the rest of England. Thus, Londoners are less likely to be admitted to a home than is assumed, but they would have more spent on them if they were admitted (compared to what we have estimated). The net effect is ambiguous, though it would probably alter the distribution slightly in favour of other regions. The effect on the distribution between income groups is unlikely to be very significant.

Local authority housing

The estimates of housing benefits in kind described above were based on a measure of the economic subsidy to individual tenants. Estimates of local authority property values, which form the basis for calculating economic subsidies, take into account the region in which the property is located, but not sub-regional variations in house prices. This may bias the distribution of benefits - make it more pro-poor than it really is - if, in fact, richer tenants are living in nicer areas within each region (and so are occupying more valuable properties than we have assumed).

Council tenants are also allocated local authority spending on maintenance and management (M&M) and an allowance for major repairs. The amount of M&M imputed to each household is an average for the region (adjusted for the size of the property) and the allowance for major repairs is just a fixed proportion of the property value (1.02%, except in Greater London). Thus, sub-regional variations in spending are not incorporated in these estimates.

Revenue allocations to local authorities, from which spending on maintenance and repairs is funded, are guided by the use of a Generalised Needs Index (GNI). The GNI includes a local authority stock condition indicator, which ensures that more funding is directed to run-down, mainly urban, areas. Since these areas are likely to include poorer-than-average tenants, ignoring these local variations would have made the distribution less pro-poor than it is, offsetting the effect of local variations in property values (see above). A small proportion of maintenance funding (10%) is distributed on the basis of an index of local conditions, which is a mix of social indicators; this, too, will favour poorer tenants. The net effect of sub-regional variations in property values and M&M spending is, therefore, ambiguous, though it is unlikely to be very large.

Summary

The potential distributional effects of local variations in spending are summarised in Table 7.6.

Table 7.6: Distributional Impact of Local Variations

	Factors not taken into account	Potential distributional impact
Regional variations		
Schools	Regional variations in unit costs	Negligible
Hospitals and community health services	Regional variations in unit costs	Marginally pro-rich
Sub-regional variations		
Schools	Needs-based variations in funding (e.g. additional education allowance)	Significantly pro-poor
Hospitals and community health services	Inclusion of health indicators in funding formulae	Moderately pro-poor?
Higher education	Differences in funding per student between institutions	Slightly pro-rich
Non-residential care	Inclusion of health indicators in funding formulae, local discretion	Slightly pro-poor?
Residential care	Local variations in admission rates and unit costs	Slightly pro-poor?
Local authority housing	Sub-regional variations in property values, targeting of M&M and major repairs spending	Net effect is ambiguous, but small

- Although there are significant *regional* variations in unit costs, their net effect on the distribution between income groups is likely to be small. This is because differences between regions are averaged out across income groups. If anything, taking differences in unit costs into account would produce a slightly more pro-rich distribution of benefits in kind. Even this weak conclusion assumes that higher unit costs reflect genuine differences in the intensity or quality of service being provided, rather than regional differences in efficiency or wage costs.

- Variations in spending *within regions* are likely to have a more significant distributional impact, because a share of government support for welfare services is specifically targeted at areas that have greater educational, health care, or housing needs, which tend also to be the poorest areas. By far the most significant effect that was not picked up in earlier analysis is the *potential* variation in spending on schools, as a result of the "additional education allowance" and the LEA formulae used to distribute these extra funds to individual schools (see Table 7.5).

- Our analysis rests on the assumption that allocated funding is a reasonable guide to actual spending, but this may not be the case. Firstly, local authorities re-allocate funding between the range of services they are responsible for, so there is no definitive link between what the formulae says is needed and what is actually spent. Secondly, even if funding is spent on the service it was designated for, it may not be spent on those people within the area who are in greatest need. This is particularly difficult to tell in the case of health care, because the distribution of benefits is determined by the purchasing decisions of Health Authorities, about which little is known yet.

Chapter Eight: Conclusions

This report examines the benefits people receive from the free or subsidised provision of public services, including the National Health Service, state education, social housing, and personal social services. It addresses three broad questions about the distribution of this "social wage":

- Who benefits most from welfare services? In particular, is there any validity to the proposition that public services have been 'captured' by the middle classes (i.e. higher income groups)?

- How has the distribution of the social wage changed since 1979? To what extent can these changes be accounted for by government policy?

- Do changes in the social wage affect conclusions about trends in income inequality over this period?

Who benefits most from welfare services?

Previous work in this area has produced two conflicting stories about the distribution of benefits from welfare services. On the one hand, the government's own analysis (by the Office of National Statistics) suggests that poorer households benefit more than richer ones from the provision of these services. On the other hand, earlier analysis by Le Grand appeared to show that the better-off were getting more than their fair share and that the welfare state had failed, at least in terms of achieving its redistributional role. Admittedly, the two analyses were not always answering the same questions. For example, Le Grand did not argue that richer people were receiving more health care than poorer people, but that they were getting more *in relation to their need*. Nevertheless, the Le Grand thesis and the ONS analysis are full of apparent contradictions. The "story" revealed in this report is closer to that told by the ONS, partly because it is answering many of the same questions. However, the story is also a more complex one than is revealed by the ONS figures and contains various sub-plots.

Our estimates show a distribution that is pro-poor throughout this period, in the sense that people in the poorest income groups receive significantly more benefits in kind from public services than people from the richest income groups. In 1993, at the end of the period, the value of the social wage going to the bottom quintile group was around 70 per cent greater than the amount going to the top quintile group. Much of this can be explained by differences in the demographic composition of income groups.

The degree of this pro-poor bias varies significantly between services. Before demographic factors have been adjusted for, housing and personal social services are both strongly pro-poor, schools (including further education) and health care are moderately pro-poor, and higher education is strongly pro-rich (see Table 8.1). Within sectors, there are important differences in the distribution of particular services. For example, higher education spending on non-mature students is more pro-rich than spending on mature students.

Table 8.1: The Distribution of Benefits In Kind, 1993

Service	Ratio of spending per person on the bottom quintile group to that on the top quintile group:	
	Actual	Demographically-adjusted
National Health Service	**1.3**	**1.1**
Short -stay hospital	1.3	1.1
GP consultations	1.3	1.2
Prescriptions	1.6	1.5
Schools and further education	**2.2**	**1.1**
Under 16	2.8	1.2
Aged 16-18	1.2	1.0
Aged 19 or over	0.8	1.1
Higher education	**0.5**	**0.7**
Aged 18-24	0.4	0.6
Aged 25 or over	0.8	1.3
Subsidised social housing	**9.9**	**6.2**
Council housing	30.1	9.0
Right To Buy scheme	1.7	2.1
Personal social services	**7.9**	**1.1**
Residential care	7.5	1.1
Non-residential care	9.1	1.1
ALL SERVICES	**1.7**	**1.2**

A list of some of the factors affecting the distribution of benefits in kind is provided in Table 8.2. The age composition of the population, in particular, has a strong influence on the shape of the distribution. Since most education spending is on children and the majority of NHS spending is on elderly people, this favours lower income groups which contain a disproportionate share of elderly people and children.

Table 8.2: Factors Affecting the Distribution of the Social Wage

Pro-poor	Ambiguous	Pro-rich
Age composition of population	Compulsion (e.g. attendance at school)	Accessibility (e.g. qualifications to enter higher education)
Other factors affecting need* (e.g. morbidity)	Cost of using services (e.g. transport, foregone pay)	Demand-led use?
Use of private sector alternatives (e.g. independent schools)		Regional variations in unit costs**
Targeting of services (e.g. council housing)		
Means-testing and charges		
Sub-regional variations in funding**		

*   taken into account indirectly through other socio-economic variables;
**   not taken into account in the main part of the analysis.

There are two reasons for regarding 'pro-poorness' that results from demographic factors differently to 'pro-poorness' that is more directly linked to people's position in the income distribution. Firstly, demographic factors are a good indicator of need for most services, including health care, education, and personal social services and there is clearly a distinction to be drawn between someone who gets more of a service because they need it more and someone who gets more because they are poorer. Secondly, everyone starts young and gets older. Over their lifetime, differences in the use of services that are related to age will be ironed out. What is left are those differences that are related to non-demographic factors.

Controlling for differences in the use of services that are related to age and gender, the pro-poor bias in the overall distribution of benefits in kind is considerably reduced (from 1.7 to 1.2), though there is still an underlying pro-poor bias. (see Table 8.1). Demographic adjustment has a greater impact on some services than others. For example, the pro-poor bias in the distribution of personal social services virtually disappears, once demographic factors are removed, implying that services are aimed primarily at elderly people in general (who also happen to be poor), rather than at the poorest among the elderly. In certain cases, such as further and higher education for mature students, a pro-rich distribution becomes pro-poor after demographic factors have been controlled for. Social housing, on the other hand, maintains its strong pro-poor bias.

Caveats

The conclusion that welfare services contain a small, but significant, pro-poor bias requires some qualification. Firstly, this does not make allowance for differences in need other than those related to age or gender, for example that children from deprived areas may need more intensive education to attain the same academic results. In relation to need, the pro-poor bias will be reduced or may disappear altogether.

On the other hand, mechanisms for allocating government funding do steer a greater share of spending to people or areas in greater need. For example, the formula for distributing funding for schools includes an allowance for "additional education needs". Taking these local variations in spending into account would compensate for some of the differences in need referred to above (see Chapter Seven).

A second caveat stems from our assumption that all users receive an equal benefit from using a particular service (e.g. that all primary-school children receive the same value of benefits in kind). However, if children from better-off families are getting into the best schools or middle class people are commanding more of their GP's time in a given visit, this would imply that the distribution is less pro-poor than we have suggested.

Finally, the way in which the results are presented in Table 8.1 conceals what is happening in the middle of the income distribution. In the case of health care and personal social services, for example, the second and third (poorest) quintile groups both receive more than the bottom quintile group, after controlling for demographic factors. If the needs of the poorest are indeed greater, this would suggest that services may not be reaching those in *greatest* need.

Distributional changes since 1979

Between 1979-93, the overall value of the social wage increased by around 30 per cent in real (RPI-adjusted) terms, which benefited all income groups. Lower income groups experienced bigger increases than higher income groups, so the distribution of the social wage has become more pro-poor over the period.

Contrary to what is often claimed, demographic changes have reduced the overall pressure on welfare services. In other words, if the same amount were spent on each age group as in 1979, then overall spending would be lower now given the changes that have taken place in the age composition of the population. This is because the effects of a falling child population - on education spending - have more than offset the effects of an ageing population - on health care and personal social services spending. However, the effects of demographic change were not uniform across income groups. The top half of the income distribution experienced a larger reduction in demographic pressures, which is the main reason why they experienced a smaller increase in benefits in kind.

Table 8.3 shows that the proportion of the social wage received by the poorest 50 per cent of the population increased by four percentage points between 1979-93. But, most of this is accounted for by demographic factors; once these are adjusted for, the share received by the poorest 50 per cent went up by less than one percentage point. This small increase in pro-poorness can be attributed to non-demographic factors, including changes in government policy.

Demographic factors have an even stronger impact on changes in the distribution of individual services. In 1993, less was being spent on the health care of the poorest half of the population than in 1979, but there was also a smaller proportion of elderly people in lower income groups. Demographically-adjusted spending on the health care of the poorest 50 per cent actually increased slightly over this period. The picture for education is the reverse. Given changes in the age composition of the population that have taken place over the period, a smaller share of resources is now being directed at the poor than in 1979.

Impact on income inequality

The social wage is fairly evenly distributed between income groups, whereas cash incomes are unequally distributed. Adding the value of benefits in kind to cash incomes will therefore have an equalising effect on the income distribution. Changes in the social wage have also affected trends in inequality over time.

On the one hand, the size of the social wage has fallen as a proportion of final incomes (cash incomes plus the social wage) from 14.0 per cent in 1979 to 13.1 per cent in 1993. This will have reduced the potential equalising effect of the social wage. On the other hand, the distribution of the social wage has become slightly more pro-poor over the period, which will have strengthened its equalising effect.

Table 8.3: Changes in Distribution of the Social Wage, 1997-93

	Share of benefits in kind received by the poorest 50 per cent of the population (%):		
	1979	1993	Change: 1979-93
I. Actual			
National Health Service	57.0	56.6	-0.4
Schools and further education	58.0	59.8	+1.8
Higher education	32.9	36.8	+3.9
Personal social services	87.4	79.3	-8.1
Social housing	61.3	75.9	+14.6
All services	**56.0**	**60.1**	**+4.1**
II. Demographically-adjusted			
National Health Service	51.3	52.6	+1.3
Schools and further education	52.7	51.8	-0.9
Higher education	49.0	44.9	-4.1
Personal social services	56.0	54.0	+2.0
Social housing	61.1	72.9	+11.8
All services	**52.9**	**53.7**	**+0.8**

Overall, inequality has increased, even if the social wage is included in the measure of income. Thus, changes in the social wage have not prevented inequality from rising. However, changes in the social wage have helped to offset the increased inequality of cash incomes. According to the standard measure of inequality, the Gini coefficient, the increase in inequality since 1979 is smaller by around one fifth, once the social wage effect is taken into account.

An increase in the disparity of incomes might be less of a concern, if all income groups were experiencing growing incomes. While the cash incomes of the bottom quintile group grew only slightly over the period (by around 6 per cent), final incomes (which include the social wage) grew by between 6-13 per cent, depending on how cost inflation is adjusted for. Only to this limited extent, can it be argued that people at the bottom of the income distribution have benefited from economic growth through higher spending on welfare services.

One factor that is not allowed for in these calculations is changing needs. The evidence on this is not clear-cut. The demographic-related needs of the bottom quintile group have slightly lessened over the period, but other factors, in particular the growth in unemployment and the growing disparity in the ability to pay for private alternatives, are likely to have increased the needs of the poor relative to the rich.

Concluding remarks

Any judgment about the distribution of the social wage will depend on initial expectations. If the expectation was that welfare services would benefit mainly lower income groups, then it may be surprising that the poorest half of the population are only receiving 60 per cent of the value of these services and only 54 per cent, once demographic effects are removed. To a large extent, services are directed at children and elderly people (who are also poorer-than-average), rather than at poorer people per se. On the other hand, the pessimistic view that public services have been captured by the middle classes is not borne out by the evidence either. All services, with the exception of higher education, have at least some pro-poor bias. On the whole, therefore, universal services are generating universal benefits with a small bias in favour of lower income groups.

Nor has the situation changed very dramatically since 1979. The distribution of the social wage has become slightly more pro-poor over the period, but again much of this can be accounted for by demographic factors. Despite the political rhetoric, there is little evidence of a smaller, more targeted, provision of welfare services. Spending on services has risen in real terms by around 30 per cent, roughly in line with the growth in GDP. This increase has benefited all income groups. Only in the case of housing has there been a very clear shift in the distribution between income groups, in favour of the poorest. In other areas, higher charges (or income-related contributions), which might have been expected to target resources more closely at the poorest, appear to have had only a marginal impact on the distribution. Where an expansion in services has taken place, for example in post-compulsory education, higher income groups have benefited as much, if not more, than lower income groups.

Appendix 1: Methodology

I. *General*

The base dataset for this analysis is the FES (Family Expenditure Survey). However, information from three other datasets is also used: the HBAI (Households Below Average Income), the GHS (General Household Survey), and the BSM (Building Society Mortgages 5 per cent sample) . These data need to be imported into the FES in order to integrate our estimates of benefits in kind into a single dataset:

- The HBAI is used for its data on household incomes, because it is the official measure employed by the DSS in their annual reports on the bottom half of the income distribution. The HBAI is itself derived from the FES, so it is straightforward to import the data on incomes back into the FES (using household identifiers). The measure of income employed throughout this report is net equivalised income, Before Housing Costs.

- The GHS provides additional information on the use of public services, in particular health care services and personal social services. This information cannot be imported directly into the FES, because it is based on a different sample of households. Regression analysis is used to relate the use of services to individual and household characteristics, including incomes. The GHS does not ask the same questions in all years, so where necessary data is used for the nearest available year.

- The BSM (now known as the Survey of Mortgage Lenders) is used to estimate regression equations for property values, using information on the characteristics of properties which is common to both the BSM and the FES.

The use of these datasets and other sources of data is summarised in Table A1.1.

Table A1.1: Data Sources for Allocation of Benefits in Kind

	Sources of data
HEALTH CARE	
NHS expenditure	Current expenditure from HoC Select Committee Report, capital expenditure from CSO (1995a)
Use of short-stay hospital services, GP consultations and prescriptions	Use of different services from GHS for nearest year (1982 GHS for 1979), length of stay data from DoH (1986) and DoH (1994)
Use of long-stay hospital services	Data from DoH (1995a) and equivalent for other years, DHSS (1984) and DoH-provided data
Use of dental, opthalmic, and Community Health Services	Age/sex breakdown from DoH (1995a) and equivalent for other years
Local variations	Regional expenditure from DoH (1995a); funding formulae from NHS Executive (1994)
PSS: RESIDENTIAL CARE	
Admissions data, mortality rates/expected length of stay	Data for residential homes from DoH (1991), DoH (1995b), DoH (1988) and OPCS (1991); data for nursing homes from Laing and Buisson (1995), Darton (1992), and OPCS (1991)
Residential care fees	Data for local authority homes from DoH (1996a); data for independent homes from CPAG (1988) and equivalents for other years
Means-test for residential care	DHSS (unpublished) for local authority homes; CPAG (1988) and Age Concern (1995) for independent homes
Local variations	Local admission rates from DoH (1991); local residential fees from DoH (1996a)
PSS: NON-RESIDENTIAL CARE	
Total expenditure by service	From DoH (1996b)
Use of home helps, day centres, and meals services	Data from GHS for nearest year (1980 GHS for 1979, 1985 GHS for 1987, and 1991 GHS for 1993)
EDUCATION	
Total expenditure by sector	Current expenditure from DfE (1995) and equivalent for other years; capital expenditure from CSO (1995a)
Primary, secondary, and tertiary sector students living at home	FES data for relevant years, cross-checked against totals from DfE (1995)
Non-residential students	Admissions data from UCAS (1994), UCCA (1992) and equivalent for other years

Calculation of maintenance payments for students	Halsbury (1993) and equivalent for other years
Local variations	Local unit costs for schools from CIPFA (1995); variation in unit costs of HE establishments from DfEE-provided data
HOUSING	
Gross imputed rents on local authority properties	Property values estimated using BSM 5% sample (for 1979 and 1987) and FES (for 1993); trended using earnings data from CSO (1996); expected rate of return from Hills (1991a)
Management and maintenance costs	Data from CIPFA (1988) and CIPFA Scottish Branch (1979) and equivalent for other years; property size differentials from DoE (1993)
Right-To-Buy households	Likely RTB households identified using FES data and cross-checked using Kerr (1988) and Gay (1990); estimated mortgage payments based on FES data and inputs from Council of Mortgage Lenders (1995), and Holmans (1990); total value of RTB subsidies based on Gay (1990) and DoE- provided data

II.   Health care

The principal source of information on the use of health care services is the General Household Survey. The GHS contains detailed questions on the use of health care services by individual household members, for example on the number of in-patient stays or GP consultations. Survey data are not available for all services, so these are supplemented by other official sources, in particular Department of Health statistical publications.

Logit equations are estimated using GHS data and applied to the FES to generate a probability for each individual that they will have used a particular service (e.g. an out-patient visit) based on their own and their household's characteristics. Other than age and gender, the main characteristics taken into account are social class, marital status, employment status, tenure, region, and income. Dummy variables are also included for disabled persons and mothers of new-born babies. The aim is to capture as far as possible those factors that affect people's need and/or demand for different health care services. Separate equations are estimated for eight age and gender groups to allow for differences in the significance of variables between these groups.

These regression equations predict the probability that someone will have used a particular service at least once. To allow for the fact that some people will have used them more than once, GHS data are used to calculate the average number of visits by age group *among patients who have had at least one visit*. The probabilities generated from the regressions are then weighted accordingly. (This gives a greater weight to older patients, who are more likely to have made multiple visits.)

A further adjustment is made for differences in the average cost of in-patient stays and prescriptions between age groups. The average cost per in-patient stay is based on the average length of hospital stays by age group, using Department of Health statistics (the In-Patient Enquiry and, for more recent years, Hospital Episodes Statistics).

Having allocated gross expenditure, charges are deducted for prescriptions and dental services. Patients who are exempt from charges (e.g. the young, the old, new mothers, and those on low incomes) are identified and total revenue from charges is then distributed to all other patients in proportion to their use of these services.

Survey information is not available on the use of all health care services, so expenditure on these services is allocated in a more ad hoc manner. For example, expenditure on school health and community midwifery is distributed evenly between all school-age children and all mothers of new-born babies respectively. Expenditure on dental services and other community health services is apportioned using an age breakdown of the use of these services from Department of Health publications.

Non-household population

Not all NHS expenditure on in-patients can be allocated on the basis of survey data, since some longer-stay in-patients are not captured in household surveys. The proportion of health care expenditure on the household population is estimated using data on the duration of stay of psychiatric and geriatric in-patients. (Acute in-patients are all assumed to be short-stay patients.) Those patients who are in hospital for longer than one year are assumed to be omitted from household surveys and patients staying for between one month and one year have some probability of being omitted.[36] Expenditure on the household population is allocated using survey data, as explained above.

---

36 FES interviewers will return to interview someone who is away from home for less than one month.

The remainder of NHS expenditure (on the non-household population) is not allocated using survey data, because we cannot assume that household surveys are representative of these patients. Instead, this expenditure is apportioned to individuals in the household population using an age breakdown of resident mentally ill, mentally handicapped, and geriatric in-patients for the nearest year available. The rationale for allocating this expenditure to the household population (even though it is not being spent on them) is that there is a potential benefit to them from having these services freely available if they were to need them. In this analysis, the risk of someone becoming a long-stay patient is based only on their age.

Administration and capital costs

Administration costs are allocated in proportion to people's use of all the services to which these costs relate. Capital costs present particular difficulties, because the value of services provided by the capital stock depend not just on capital expenditure in the current year, but also on capital expenditure in previous years. To reflect this, a weighted average of past capital spending is calculated - over thirty years for buildings and over five years for equipment.[37] This, too, is allocated in proportion to people's overall use of health care services.

III. Housing

Local authority tenants

People living in local authority housing benefit from rents that are lower than economic rents - defined as the level of rents that would be need to be charged if local authorities were to cover their costs in full. To measure this subsidy, we estimate economic rents and deduct the rents actually charged by local authorities.

The methodology used in this and previous studies is to calculate economic rents as a fixed proportion of property values plus or minus various adjustments for upkeep, depreciation, and capital gains. The rationale is that the return on housing (including the flow of housing services) should be comparable to the return available on similar capital assets. The formula for calculating economic rents is as follows:

---

37   One quarter of capital spending on the NHS is assumed to be spent on buildings and three quarters on equipment.

Economic rent	= estimated property value x required rate of return
	- expected capital gain + depreciation
	+ maintenance and management costs

Information is not available on the value of local authority properties, so these need to be estimated, based on the values of comparable properties in the owner-occupied sector. This is done by means of regression analysis, using FES data on the characteristics of individual properties (including the number of rooms, whether it has a garage, its location, and rateable value[38] or council tax band). In 1993, information is also provided on the purchase price of owner-occupied properties, so the regression analysis is carried out on the FES sub-sample of owner-occupied properties and applied to the sub-sample of local authority households. In other years, there are no FES data on property values, even for owner-occupiers. Therefore, the regression equations for 1979 and 1987 are estimated using another survey - the DoE's Building Society Mortgages 5 per cent sample. This contains data on the purchase price of newly-mortgaged properties, as well as information on the charateristics of properties. The set of independent variables is limited to information that is common to both the BSM and the FES.

One problem with this type of analysis is that the regression equations are unlikely to capture all those factors that influence the value of a property. For example, location is very important in determining property values, but the only locational variable in our equations is the region, which does not distinguish properties in Brixton from those in Chelsea, for example. Nor, do our equations contain a variable for the condition of the property. This would not matter too much if the resulting errors were likely to be random or non-systematic. But, in this case, we might expect local authority properties to be in worse locations and in worse condition than otherwise similar properties in the owner-occupied sector. Thus, our regression estimates would tend to over-state the value of the local authority stock.

---

38 Rateable value is a key variable in the 1979 and 1987 equations. The 1987 FES includes data on calculated rate payments, but *not* on rateable values. The latter are estimated by combining data on rate payments with imputed rate poundages, based on the region and the type of administrative area (i.e. Greater London, metropolitan, non-metropolitan, rural, very rural) in which the household lives.

Fortunately, the BSM identifies buyers who are sitting tenant purchasers (i.e. former local authority tenants). The benefit of having ex-local authority properties in the sample is that it enables us to pick up any price differential between local authority and owner-occupied properties that is not already captured by other variables in the equation. In practice, the coefficient on the "Right To Buy" dummy variable will represent a lower-bound estimate of the price differential between local authority and owner-occupied properties, since RTB properties are generally in better condition and/or in better locations than the average local authority property. Since there were no RTB properties in the 1979 BSM (because the scheme had not yet begun), the coefficients in that year are based on the 1987 BSM. (This assumes that the *relative* values of local authority and owner-occupied authorities did not change over this period.) In 1993, the regression equations are based on the FES which does not identify RTB properties. However, information is available that allows us to identify likely RTB households (see below), from which the value of the RTB dummy variable is estimated.

In 1987, the value of local authority properties are discounted by 18 per cent (and by more in Greater London) and in 1993, they are discounted by around 12 per cent. The reduction in the discount between the two years does not necessarily mean that local authority properties have increased in value relative to owner-occupied properties. An alternative explanation is that other variables included in the regression equations are 'doing more of the work' in 1993 than in 1987. For example, council tax bands (included in the 1993 equation) may be capturing more of the differences in the value of properties than were rateable values (included in the 1987 equation), which by the mid-1980s were becoming a poorer guide to actual property values.

Having estimated current property values, these are 'trended', so that our measure of economic subsidy does not fluctuate widely in line with actual house prices. We assume that trend house prices are linked to the growth in male earnings over this period. The rationale is that in the long-run, house prices cannot rise much faster than earnings or else housing would be become unaffordable. The effect of trending is to scale down estimates of property values in 1987 (compared to 1979) and to scale up estimates in 1993. Thus, changes in average house prices are linked to the growth in male earnings, but changes in relative house prices (between different types of property) are captured by the regression equations.

The required rate of return on the estimated property value is based on the average return on 10-year index-linked gilts during the

1980s, which was around 4%. This is less than the returns apparently sought by landlords in the private rented sector and less than the assumption used by government in calculating the Tenanted Market Value of local authority properties (8% real). One justification for using a lower rate of return is that the required rate of return for private sector landlords includes a substantial risk premium. For example, landlords face the risk of sudden changes in the value of their property, the risk of a reversion to a less favourable regulatory environment for private renting, the risk of their tenants defaulting on payments, and the risk of a property being left vacant while a suitable tenant is found. It is not appropriate to include this risk premium in estimating imputed returns to local authority tenants, because their 'return' in the form of the services provided by the property (i.e. shelter, warmth, etc) is not subject to risks in the same way as the financial returns to private landlords.

Expected capital gains, assumed to be 1% of property values per annum, are deducted from the required rate of return. To this is added an allowance for depreciation, structural insurance, and maintenance and management costs. Depreciation is measured by the cost of major repairs, which are designed to offset the effects of depreciation. The assumptions used are the same as those employed by the Housing Corporation in their Housing Association Grant (HAG) model; these are 0.094% of estimated property values in Greater London and 1.02% elsewhere. Structural insurance costs are estimated at 0.2% of property values, which is the assumption used in a recent DSS paper on "With Housing Income" measures of income.

Estimates of maintenance and management (M&M) costs are based on actual expenditure per dwelling by region, using CIPFA data. (Special supervision and management costs are included net of service charges.) A further adjustment is made to maintenance costs to reflect the positive relationship between expenditure and property size. These are based on DoE figures for the relative cost of maintaining different sized properties (using data from the English House Condition Survey). Management costs, on the other hand, are assumed not to vary with property size.

To estimate the net economic subsidy to social rented sector tenants, actual rents are deducted from our estimates of economic rents. Our definition of actual rent is the rent charged (before deducting housing benefit and rate rebates) *less* council tax or rates payments where these are included in rents. The reason for deducting local taxes and charges for utilities (e.g. water rates) is that these payments are for non-housing services, the benefits of which are not included in our estimates of economic rent.

The Right To Buy scheme

The policy of selling off council houses, mainly under the Right To Buy scheme, has significantly reduced the number of local authority tenants and therefore the number of people receiving subsidies in the form of sub-economic rents. However, one form of subsidy has been replaced by a different kind of subsidy - subsidised owner-occupation. In addition, to mortgage interest tax relief (which is already counted in HBAI incomes), Right To Buy purchasers benefit from a significant discount on the purchase price of their property.

The first and biggest problem in allocating the benefits of the Right To Buy scheme is to identify those households who bought their home under the scheme. Given that the FES does not ask any direct questions about participation in the RTB scheme, this has to be deduced using information that is given in the FES on length of residence, date of purchase, and mortgage payments. Certain criteria can be established for narrowing down the group of possible RTBers based on what we know about the scheme's conditions. Possible RTBers are identified as households who:

- bought their current home in or after 1980 (when the RTB scheme was introduced); and

- were living in their current home for at least two years before they bought it (i.e. the qualifying period); and whose

- original mortgage is significantly below the estimated value of the property at the date of purchase (by an amount that is roughly equal to the eligible discount plus the average deposit on new mortgages).

The first two criteria are relatively straightforward to apply. But, these two criteria are not sufficient in themselves, because they do not rule out owner-occupiers who rented their home in the private sector before purchasing it or people who have bought from a relative they have been living with. However, the calculations involved in testing the third criteria are subject to quite large margins of error. For example, households may be wrongly classified as RTB households if they put down a much larger-than-average deposit on their mortgage (which will make the value of their mortgage low relative to the value of their property). Hopefully, these errors will be fairly random and so should not unduly bias the *distribution* of RTB households between income groups.[39] But, it is too much to assume that this methodology will

147

correctly predict the *number* of RTB households and therefore the overall *value* of RTB subsidies. This is corrected for later on.

The subsidy to RTB household comes in the form of a discount on the purchase price of their home. This could be treated as a once-off lump sum benefit and allocated in full to the RTB household in the year they purchased. An alternative approach adopted in this analysis is to annualise the value of the subsidy over time. RTB households are allocated the economic rent on that part of their property that was discounted (i.e. the current value of the property multiplied by the discount they would have been eligible for multiplied by the rate of return on this equity). The rate of return is the same as the one used for local authority tenants (i.e. 3.5-4.5%)

The amount allocated to RTB households is calibrated using a separate estimate of the total value of RTB subsidies. This is based on aggregate data from official publications and the Department of the Environment on the number of RTB sales, the average value of these properties, and the average discount.

Equivalisation

Benefits in kind from housing are calculated on a *per household* basis, so they need to be converted to a *per person* basis to make them comparable with the value of other benefits in kind. In the absence of a specific equivalence scale for housing, the McClements scale is used. Appendix 3 provides a sensitivity analysis to the use of alternative equivalence scales.

IV. Personal Social Services

Only expenditure on elderly people is allocated, largely for practical reasons. In the case of non-residential care, the GHS questions on the use of personal social services are only addressed to those aged over 65. In the case of residential care, the amount of support received depends on a person's income; only for retired persons is it reasonable to assume that current income (as reported in the survey) is representative of the person's income if were they to enter a residential home.

---

39 Other characteristics of households identified as likely Right To Buyers (e.g. the age distribution of the heads of household) are fairly consistent with the findings of special DoE surveys of actual RTB participants (Kerr, 1988).

Non-residential care

The allocation of expenditure on domiciliary services is very similar to that for health care services. Again, GHS data are used to estimate the probability of someone using a particular service based on their age, gender, marital status, and other characteristics. These regressions are applied to the FES data set and expenditure is allocated accordingly. Expenditure is distributed evenly between all users, since there is insufficient information on the intensity of use by different types of client. Charges for these services are discretionary, so that policies vary between local authorities. However, there are statutory guidelines, including a requirement to take into account people on low incomes. As a crude simplification, charges are deducted from all users, except those on Income Support.

Residential care

The rationale for allocating expenditure on residential care (even though the recipients do not appear in household surveys) is the same as for long-stay hospital patients. Expenditure on residential care is allocated using an insurance-based approach:

- individuals (in the household population) are assigned a probability of entering a residential or nursing home in that year based on their age and gender; and

- the probability of entering a home is multiplied by the value of the financial support they would receive as a resident *over the full expected duration of their stay* (which may be several years).

The probability of someone entering a home is based on Department of Health admissions data, which provide a break down of the number of people admitted to different types of home by broad age groups (aged 65-74, 75-84, and over 85). The admissions data do not identify men and women seperately, so our gender split is based on stock data (using Census data and a special Department of Health survey in 1988). The number of people admitted in a particular age and gender group is divided by the total number of people in that age and gender group to generate a probability of being admitted in that year. (This does not take into account other factors, such as marital status or social class, which previous studies have suggested may also have an influence on the decision to enter a home.) Since admissions data are not available on nursing homes, admissions are estimated by dividing stock data by the average length of stay.

The second step is to work out the amount of financial support each person would receive under the prevailing system if they were admitted to a residential home. The amount of support that would be received is calculated by replicating the means-test used by local authorities (for their homes) and by the Department of Social Security (for independent residential and nursing homes). This requires information on people's income and their capital (which is estimated using FES data on the amount of interest earned on different assets). The estimated value of a person's own home (less 10% for costs and less the value of the mortgage) is counted as capital if that person is not sharing their house with a close relative (i.e. if their property would have to be sold to pay for residential care).

However, the insurance value of residential care provision has to be calculated not just for that year, but over the full expected duration of stay. This requires information on the likely length of stay of newly admitted residents. Since limited data are available on completed lengths of stay in residential homes, these are inferred from estimates of mortality rates (see Box below). No admissions data are available for independent homes before 1993, so mortality rates are assumed to be the same as for independent homes in 1993 and admissions are imputed (using the calculations in the Box, but in reverse).

The level of support in the second and subsequent years is worked out by repeating the original means-test, but allowing for the run-down of capital assets (where charges exceed a person's income). The value of support in later years is then discounted (at a rate of 8% per annum) and multiplied by the probability that someone would survive for the extra year (i.e. one minus their estimated mortality rate). This enables us to calculate a figure for the expected net present value of residential care support for each person over 65 if admitted in that year. Multiplying this figure by the probability of being admitted produces an estimate for the insurance value to each individual of the present system of financial support.

There is no reason why these insurance values, totalled over the survey population, should be equal to actual expenditure on residential care. One reason is that the incomes of people in the household population may be different from the incomes of people in residential homes (which matters because financial support is means-tested). Another reason is that actual expenditure depends on the stock of residents, whereas insurance values are based on the number of admissions in a particular year.

Calculation of Mortality Rates in Residential Homes

$$DEATHS^{55-64} = \left[\frac{87STOCK^{55-64} - 88STOCK^{55-64} + ADM^{55-64} - TRANS^{55-64} - (0.1 * 87STOCK)^{55-64}}{(1-0.1)} \right]$$

$$MORT^{55-64} = \frac{DEATHS^{55-64}}{(87STOCK^{55-64} + 88STOCK^{55-64})/2} * 1000$$

$$DEATHS^{65-74} = \left[\frac{87STOCK^{65-74} - 88STOCK^{65-74} + ADM^{65-74} - TRANS^{65-74} - (0.1*87STOCK)^{65-74} + (0.1*87STOCK^{65-74} * MORT^{65-74}}{(1-0.1)} \right]$$

$$MORT^{65-74} = \frac{DEATHS^{65-74}}{(87STOCK^{65-74} + 88STOCK^{65-74})/2} * 1000$$

etc...

Where:

$DEATHS^{x-y}$	= number of deaths aged x to y
$87STOCK^{x-y}$	= stock of residents aged x to y in year 87
ADM^{x-y}	= number of new admissions aged x to y
$TRANS^{x-y}$	= number of residents transferred to other sectors (negative for inflows)
$MORT^{x-y}$	= mortality rate for residents aged x to y (per thousand residents)

V. Education

Expenditure on schools is relatively straightforward to allocate, because the FES separately identifies students at special, primary, and secondary state schools. Tertiary education is more complicated, partly because a significant proportion of students living in halls of residence are not covered in household surveys. A more conceptual problem is whether expenditure should be allocated to students or to their parents.

Schools

Public expenditure on primary schools is distributed evenly among all primary school students (excluding those at independent schools) and similarly for expenditure on special and secondary state schools. No attempt is made in the main part of the report to take account of local variations in spending per pupil, which are discussed in Chapter Seven. Other related expenditure, for example on school transport, is not allocated.

Capital spending on schools, as for health care, is calculated as a weighted average of past capital spending (averaged over five years for equipment and over twenty years for buildings). It is then distributed in proportion to current expenditure on each pupil.

Tertiary education

The biggest difficulty in allocating expenditure on tertiary education is that a large number of non-resident students are missing from household surveys. Since the FES does not identify households with non-resident students, we use admissions data collected by PCAS and UCCA (now merged into UCAS); this provides a breakdown of acceptances to universities and former-polytechnics by social class. The number of students in each social class who are living at home (and therefore included in household surveys) is deducted from these totals to give the number of non-resident students by social class. Heads of household aged between 42-60 are then assigned a probability of having a non-resident student based on their social class.

These probabilities are added to the information already available on students living at home and used to apportion government expenditure on higher education (including tuition fees, but excluding maintenance payments). Some allowance is made for the fact that mature students are less likely than younger students to be doing their first degree and so may not be eligible for Mandatory Awards to cover their tuition fees.

The same methodology cannot be applied to further education establishments, because information on the social class of these students is not available. Thus, expenditure on these establishments is distributed between students who are living at home. This is not too problematic because a far greater proportion of further education students do live at home.

Although maintenance payments are a form of cash income, they are not fully reflected in HBAI incomes, because many of the recipients (i.e. non-resident students) are missing from the survey. The value of maintenance payments is therefore imputed using the grant formula set out in legislation (which is revised annually). The size of maintenance payments depends on parental income, whether there are other dependents in the household, and whether the student is living at home or not. These values are adjusted so that the total amount allocated is equal to actual expenditure on maintenance payments. Discretionary awards are not allocated, because by their very nature there are no rules for determining how much potential recipients are eligible to receive.

VI. *Standardising for Age and Gender*

The use of most welfare services is closely associated with people's age and gender, so the distribution of benefits in kind is very sensitive to changes in the demographic composition of the population, and of particular income groups.

In this report, the distribution of spending on services is often adjusted for differences related to age and gender to help identify that part of the distribution that can be accounted for by other, non-demographic, factors.

Age/sex standardisation is carried out in the following way:

$$X^* = X - \overline{X}^{a,s} + \overline{X}$$

where: X^* = age/sex standardised expenditure

X = unadjusted expenditure

$\overline{X}^{a,s}$ = average expenditure for the age/gender group to which the individual belongs

$\overline{X}$ = average expenditure for whole population.

Appendix 2: Sensitivity Analysis

I.   Differential use of private health care

In estimating health care benefits in kind, the use of private health care had to be ignored, because the necessary microdata were not available for the end of the period. Thus, all visits to hospital were assumed to be under the NHS. This will not have affected the average level of benefits in kind (which was tied to total NHS expenditure), but it will have affected the distribution of these benefits in two ways:

- People in higher income groups generally make greater use of private health care. Taking this into account would generate a more pro-poor distribution of benefits from the NHS in each of the years examined;

- The size of the private health care market has increased significantly over the period. In 1983, 4.5 million persons were covered by private health care insurance. By 1993, this had gone up to nearly 6 million. Therefore, the effect identified above is likely to be stronger at the end than at the beginning of the period. Our analysis will not have picked up this shift in favour of lower income groups over time.

The importance of the first effect is examined using data from 1987. Table A2.1 shows the proportion of hospital visits that were taken privately in that year. The differences between income groups are very significant, especially for in-patient stays.

Table A2.1: Use of Private Health Care Services by Income Group, 1987

Proportion of visits taken privately	Quintile group (by net equivalised income)					
	Bottom	2	3	4	5	All
In-patient stays	1.6%	1.8%	3.3%	6.9%	20.0%	5.9%
Out-patient visits	1.6%	1.6%	2.7%	2.2%	6.8%	2.8%

The overall effect on the distribution of health care benefits in kind is smaller than suggested by these figures because, in most cases, people who are privately insured continue to use other NHS services (e.g. General Practioners, prescriptions, and community health services). Estimates of the distributional impact are presented in Figure A2.1. This shows that adjusting for the differential use of private health care does produce a more pro-poor distribution, but the effect is quite small. This effect may have become slightly more significant by 1993 as the number of people insured privately increased (although this depends on where new policy holders are positioned in the income distribution).

Figure A2.1: Impact of Private Health Care on the Distribution of Health Care, 1987

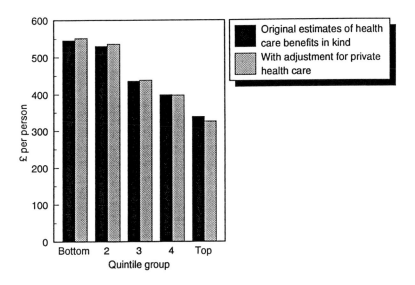

II.   *Housing association tenants*

Subsidies to housing association tenants were not included in the main analysis, because earlier FESs do not distinguish this group of tenants from private rented sector tenants. Again, for the sake of consistency, these subsidies are ignored throughout the period rather than included in some years, but not others. This is a potentially significant omission. In 1993, around 3 per cent of all households were housing association tenants, compared to around 20 per cent who were local authority tenants.

This sector has expanded rapidly since 1979 as the government has chanelled most of its funding for new build into housing associations (through the Housing Corporation's Approved Development Programme). The sector has also grown as a result of some local authorities transferring their whole stock to newly-formed housing associations as part of the Large Scale Voluntary Transfer programme. (In 1979, only about 2 per cent of households were housing association tenants.) Thus, the overall value of subsidies to housing association tenants would be greater at the end of the period than at the beginning (assuming that average subsidies per household have not fallen substantially).

The size of these subsidies is calculated for 1993, employing the same basic methodology used for estimating the subsidies to local authority tenants. The same discount is applied to the value of housing association properties as was applied to local authority properties (i.e. based on the value of Right To Buy properties relative to comparable properties in the owner-occupied sector). This may under-estimate the value of housing association properties relative to local authority properties, since they are likely to be in better condition, on average. (For example, the 1991 English House Condition Survey showed that 45 per cent of the housing association stock was in the "best condition", while only 23 per cent of the local authority stock was in that category.) Maintenance and management costs are imputed using the schedule employed by the Housing Corporation.

Figure A2.2 shows the impact of including benefits in kind to housing association tenants by income group. (The figures for local authority tenants and RTB households are mid-point estimates between the 'high' and 'low' figures reported in Chapter 4). The effect is a small, but significant, addition to the value of housing benefits in kind (of around 8 per cent in total). There is little impact on the distribution between income groups, because benefits in kind to housing association tenants have a similar pro-poor distribution to that for local authority tenants.

Table A2.2 compares the average value of economic subsidies to local authority and housing association properties in 1993. According to these estimates, the average subsidy is greater for local authority properties. Although housing association properties are worth more on average, and therefore have a higher *gross* imputed rent, this is more than offset by the higher rents paid by housing association tenants. Maintenance and management spending per dwelling is about the same. However, this result is sensitive to the assumption that the value of housing association properties should be discounted to the same extent as the value of local authority properties (i.e. by around 12 per cent). If only half this discount were applied, then the net economic subsidy on housing association properties, as calculated in Table A2.2, would be £730 per annum, and if no discount were applied it would be £850 per annum (i.e. about the same as for local authority properties).

Figure A2.2: Value of Benefits In Kind to People Living in Housing Association Properties, 1993

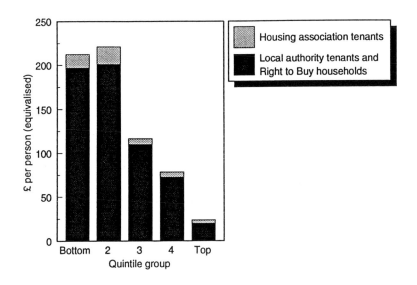

Table A2.2: Economic Subsidies to Housing Association and Local Authority Tenants, 1993

	Average for three-bedroomed properties outside Greater London	
	Local authority sector	Housing association sector
Gross imputed rent:		
Average property value	37,300	43,500
Imputed rent (4.2% of above)	1,570	1,830
M&M expenditure (£ per annum):	970	920
Gross rent (£ per annum):	1,700	2,140
Net economic subsidy (£ per annum):	840	610

III. Alternative equivalence scales for cash incomes

The McClements scale used in this and the HBAI report to equivalise people's cash incomes is just one of many different equivalence scales. The sensitivity of the HBAI figures to using alternative equivalence

157

scales is tested each year and the key results appear to be relatively unaffected by the particular scale used. However, the equivalence scale assumption can have a substantial impact on the position of particular groups in the income distribution, in particular retired households. Since elderly people are among the heaviest users of public services, this might significantly alter the distribution of the social wage.

This section examines the effects on the distribution of benefits in kind of using two of the extreme equivalence scales tested by the DSS, one of which assumes fewer economies of scale than the McClements scale (Variant 1) and the other which assumes greater economies of scale (Variant 4). Retired people generally live in smaller-than-average households, so they appear better off relative to familes when fewer economies of scale are assumed and worse off when greater economies of scale are assumed. Thus, Variant 1 pushes elderly people up the income distribution and Variant 4 pushes them further down the distribution. The resulting distribution of benefits in kind is presented in Figure A2.3.

The distribution of the social wage, as a whole, is remarkably robust to changes in the equivalence scale. The distribution is slightly more pro-poor using Variant 4, but the effect is quite small. The reason for this is that as elderly people move in and out of the bottom group, the effect on health care spending is offset by the effect on education spending. For example, under Variant 4, there are more elderly people in the bottom income group, so more is spent on health care, but there are also fewer children, so less is spent on education. Thus, the choice of equivalence scale affects the composition of the social wage by income group, but not the overall distribution.

IV. Alternative equivalence scales for housing

Housing is shared by households, which raises the question as to how the value of housing benefits in kind should be shared out between household members. The approach taken in the main part of this report was to equivalise the value of the subsidy using the McClements scale, which is the same scale used for adjusting cash incomes for differences in household size. This section explores the sensitivity of our results to two alternative assumptions:

- per capita basis: divide the value of benefits in kind equally between all household members, without allowing for any economies of scale; and

Figure A2.3: Sensitivity to Alternative Equivalence Scales for Cash Incomes, 1993

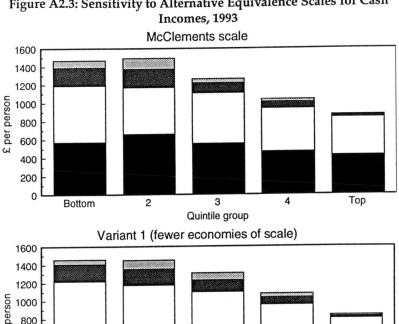

McClements scale

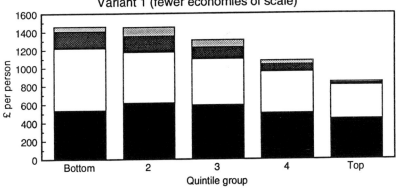

Variant 1 (fewer economies of scale)

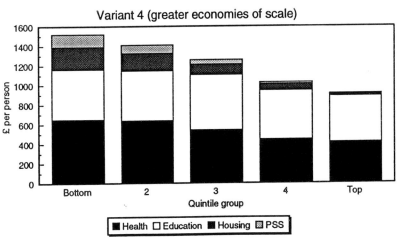

Variant 4 (greater economies of scale)

■ Health □ Education ■ Housing ▨ PSS

- no equivalisation: allocate the full value of benefits in kind to all household members, effectively assuming complete economies of scale.

The distribution of housing benefits in kind in 1993 is re-calculated using these alternative assumptions and compared to the estimates produced using the McClements scale (see Figure A2.4). The shape of the distributions are similar. The only significant difference is that the value of benefits in kind to the bottom income group is greater *relative to other income groups* when benefits are not equivalised and smaller when benefits are calculated on a per capita basis. This is because the average size of households living in local authority properties is greater for those in the bottom income group than for other income groups, so that the bottom income group is most affected by equivalisation.

The major differences are in the average value of benefits in kind, which range from £90 per person (on a per capita basis) to £230 per person (with no equivalisation). This is not surprising given that the average size of households is between 2-3. Our estimates (using the McClements scale) lie between the two extremes, though towards the lower end of the range.

Further work would be needed to produce an equivalence scale that was specific to housing. However, it seems unlikely that it would be very different from the McClements scale. Support for this is implicit in the social security system, which uses almost identical personal allowances and premiums for calculating both Income Support and Housing Benefit. The implication is that the effect of household composition on the need for cash income is similar to its effect on the need for housing services. It follows that a similar equivalence scale should be used for both cash incomes and housing. An advantage in using the *same* scale for cash incomes and housing benefits in kind is that it ensures that the treatment of housing subsidies *in kind* is consistent with the treatment of housing subsidies *in cash form* (i.e. Housing Benefit).

Figure A2.4: Sensitivity to Alternative Equivalence Scales for Housing Benefits In Kind, 1993

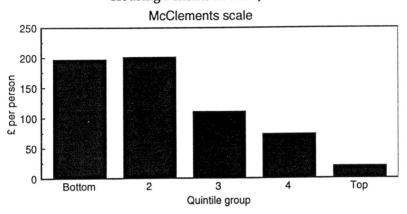

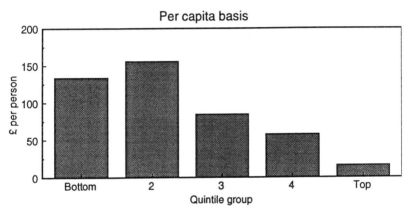

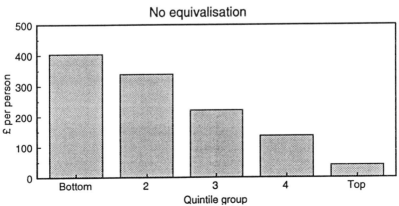

Appendix 3: Indicators of Morbidity

One of the reasons that NHS spending is likely to be pro-poor is that, other things being equal, poorer people are expected to have higher rates of morbidity (or ill-health) than richer people. This matters, because:

- If we are adjusting for differences in need, then differences in morbidity between income groups should be taken into account, as well as differences in demographic composition. The conclusions to this report showed that the distribution of benefits in kind (including health care) is pro-poor, even after adjusting for demographic factors (see Figure 8.2). But, the same conclusion may not hold true if other factors affecting need (other than age and gender) are also controlled for;

- Changes in morbidity over time may explain changes in the distribution of health care spending between income groups (see Figure 3.6).

Unfortunately, there is no easy way to measure morbidity. Figure A3.1 shows changes in three indicators of *self-reported* morbidity, taken from the General Household Survey. These figures have been adjusted for differences related to age and gender to make them comparable with Figures 3.6 and 8.2.

As expected, there is a pro-poor bias to the various indicators of (self-reported) morbidity, particularly for the more general indicator of "bad health". Self-reported morbidity is greatest among people in the second quintile group, whichever indicator is used. Thus, differences in morbidity between income groups are consistent with the pro-poor, but hump-shaped, distribution of age-adjusted NHS expenditure in 1993 (see Figure 8.2). Of course, these kinds of indicators cannot be used to assess how much of the pro-poor bias can be explained by differences in morbidity. (This would require a further judgment to be made as to the additional medical requirements of someone who has a long-standing illness or someone who has generally been in "bad health".)

However, changes in morbidity between income groups do not appear to explain why there has been a shift in NHS spending in favour of the second and third quintile groups (see Figure 3.6). For each indicator in Figure A3.1, the increase in morbidity between 1979-93 was greater for the bottom income group than for either the second or third

Figure A3.1: Indicators of Self-Reported Morbidity by Income Group, 1979-93 (adjusted for differences related to age and gender)

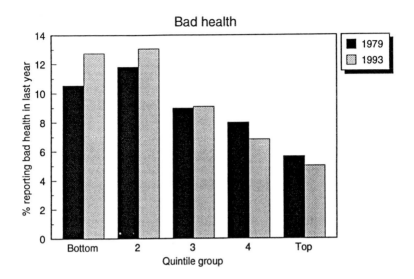

quintile groups. Yet, the bottom income group experienced a reduction in spending relative to other income groups *after adjusting for demographic factors*. The only other explanation is that changes in NHS policy over this period worked against the bottom quintile group and in favour of the second and third quintile groups. (This assumes that self-reported morbidity is a good proxy for actual morbidity, which may not be the case. For example, the willingness to report ill-health may vary over time and between age groups, social classes, regions, and genders.)

The other noticeable change over this period was the general increase in self-reported morbidity. This cannot be accounted for by an ageing population, because morbidity increased within age groups, too. Either people have become more willing to report ill-health, or detection of medical problems has improved, or people have become less healthy. If it is the latter, then adjusting for changes in morbidity since 1979 would reduce the overall growth in needs-adjusted spending.

References and bibliography

Age Concern (1995), *'Local authority charging procedures for residential and nursing home care'*, Fact Sheet No.10, London: Age Concern

Age Concern (1996), *'Preserved rights to Income Support for residential and nursing homes'*, Fact Sheet No.11, London: Age Concern

Association of British Insurers (1993), *Insurance Statistics Year Book 1983-93*, London: ABI

Balloch, S and Robertson, G (1995), *Charging for Social Care*, London: National Institute for Social Work: Local government Anti-Poverty Unit

Barclay, Sir Peter (1995), *Income and Wealth, Volume 1.* York: Joseph Rowntree Foundation

Central Statistical Office [CSO] (1994a), 'The effects of taxes and benefits on household income, 1993', *Economic Trends*, December, pp.35-73, London: HMSO

CSO (1994b), *Family Spending 1993*, London: Central Statistical Office

CSO (1994c), *General Household Survey*, London: HMSO

CSO (1995a), *United Kingdom National Accounts 1994*, London: HMSO

CSO (1995b), *Annual Abstract of Statistics 1994*, London: HMSO

CSO (1995c), *Financial Statistics*, London: HMSO

CSO (1996), *Regional Trends 30*, 1995 Edition, London: HMSO

Child Poverty Action Group [CPAG] (1988), *National Welfare Benefits Handbook*, Seventeenth edition 1987/8, London: Child Poverty Action Group

Chartered Institute of Public Finance and Accountancy [CIPFA] (1980), *Housing Revenue Account Statistics 1979/80 Actuals*, London: CIPFA

CIPFA (1988), *Rate Collection Statistics 1987/88 (Actuals)*, London: CIPFA

CIPFA (1995), *Handbook of Education Unit Costs 1993-4*, London: HMSO

CIPFA Scottish Branch (1979), *Rating Review*, 34th Year of Issue, Edinburgh: CIPFA

Cooper, A and Nye, A (1995), 'The Rowntree Inquiry and "trickle down", *HardData*, No.1. London: Social Market Foundation

Council of Mortgage Lenders (1995), *Housing Finance*, No.25, London: Building Societies Association

Darton, R (1992), *'Length of Stay of Residents and Patients in Residential and Nursing Homes: Statistical Report*, Discussion Paper 855/2, Canterbury: University of Kent, PSSRU

Department of Education and Science [DES] (1995), *Education Statistics for the United Kingdon*, 1994 Edition, London: HMSO

Department for Education [DfE] (1995), *Education Expenditure Since 1979-80*, Issue No.5/95, London: HMSO

Department of the Environment [DoE] (1993), *English House Condition Survey 1991*, London: HMSO

DoE (1995a), *Housing and Construction Statistics 1984-94: Great Britain*, London: HMSO

DoE (1995b), *Research on an Economic Model of Rent Determination in the Private Rented Sector*, London: HMSO

DoE (1996), *Simple Average House Price Index, 4th Quarter 1995*, London: HMSO

Department of Health [DoH] (1986), *Hospital In-patient Enquiry: in-patient and day case trends*, London: HMSO

DoH (1988), *Survey of age, sex and length of stay characteristics of residents of homes for elderly people and younger people who are physically handicapped in England at 31st March 1988*, London: HMSO

DoH (1991), *Residential Accommodation for Elderly and for Younger Physically Handicapped People: All Residents in Local Authority, Volunatary and Private Homes, Year Ending 31 March 1991, England*, London: HMSO

DoH (1994), *NHS hospital activity statistics: England 1983 to 1993-4*, Statistical Bulletin, London: Department of Health

DoH (1995a), *Health and Personal Social Services Statistics 1994*, London: HMSO

DoH (1995b), *Residential Accommodation for all client groups: Admissions to Local authority, volumtary and Private Homes, 1994, England*, London: HMSO

DoH (1996a), *Key Indicators of Local Authority Social Services 1995*, London: Department of Health

DoH (1996b), *Personal Social Services: A Historical Profile of Reported Current and Capital Expenditure 1983-4 to 1993-4 England*, London: HMSO

Department of Health and Social Security [DHSS] (1984), *Mental Health Statistics for England 1983-4*, London: DHSS

DHSS (unpublished), *Residential Homes Under Part III of the National Assistant Act Charging and Assessment Procedures: A memorandum of guidance*, mimeo

Department of Social Security [DSS] (1994), *Households Below Average Income: a statistical analysis 1979-1992/3*, London: HMSO

DSS (unpublished), *With Housing Measure of Incomes*, mimeo

Evandrou, M, Falkingham, J, Hills, J and Le Grand, J (1992), *The Distribution of Welfare Benefits in Kind*, STICERD Welfare State Discussion Paper WSP/68, London: London School of Economics

Evandrou, M, Falkingham, J, Le Grand, J and Winter, D (1992), 'Equity in Health and Social Care', *Journal of Social Policy*, Vol.21, No.4.

Evandrou, M, Falkingham, J, Hills, J and Le Grand, J (1993), 'Welfare benefits in kind and income distribution', *Fiscal Studies*, vol.14, pp.57-76

Evans, M (1995), *Out for the Count: The incomes of the non-household population and the effect of their exclusion from national income profiles*, STICERD Welfare State Discussion Paper WSP/111, London: London School of Economics

Falkingham, J and Hills, J (eds.) (1995), *The Dynamic of Welfare: The welfare state and the life cycle*. Hemel Hempstead: Harvester Wheatsheaf

Gardiner, K, Hills, J, Falkingham, J, Lechene, V and Sutherland, H (1995), *The Effects of Differences in Housing and Health Care Systems on International Comparisons of Income Distribution*, STICERD Welfare State Programme Discussion Paper WSP/110, London: London School of Economics

Gay, O (1990), *The Right To Buy*, Background Paper No.258, London: House of Commons Library

Goodin, R and Le Grand, J (1987), *Not only the Poor: The middle classes and the welfare state*, London: Allen and Unwin

Glennerster, H (1992), *Paying for Welfare: The 1990s*, Hemel Hempstead: Harvester Wheatsheaf

Halsbury (1993), *Halsbury's Statutes of England and Wales*, fourth edition, London: Butterworth

Henry, J, Donald, C and MacPherson, A, with Donald, K, Watkins, J and Guest, C (1993), *Survey of nursing homes in the English Counties*, London: Association of County Councils

Hills, J (ed.) (1990), *The State of Welfare: The welfare state in Britain since 1974*, Oxford: Clarendon Press

Hills, J (1991a), *Unravelling Housing Finance: Subsidies, Benefits and Taxation*, Oxford: Clarendon Press

Hills, J (1991b), *Hedonic Price Indices for Housing Derived from the 1988 5 per cent Survey of Building Society Mortgages*, STICERD Welfare State Programme Research Note WSP/RN/21, London: London School of Economics

Hills, J (1993), *The Future of Welfare: A guide to the debate*, York: Joseph Rowntree Foundation

Hills, J (1995), *Income and Wealth, Volume 2*, York: Joseph Rowntree Foundation

Hills, J (ed.) (1996), *New Inequalities: The changing distribution of income and wealth in the United Kingdom*, Cambridge: Cambridge University Press

Holmans, A (1990), *House Prices: changes through time at national and sub-national level*, Government Economic Service Working Paper No.110, London: Department of the Environment

Housing Corporation (1993), *Revised Housing Association administrative allowances for 1993/4*, Circular HC 16/93, London: Housing Corporation

House of Commons Social Services Select Committee (1989/90), Public Expenditure on Health Matters, Paper HC(1989/89)484, London: HMSO

Jenkins, S (1991), *Non-Cash and Cash Income in the UK*, unpublished

Kerr, M (1988), *The Right to Buy: A national survey of tenants and buyers of council homes for the Department of the Environment*, London: HMSO

King's Fund Institute (1994), *Health Care UK: an annual review of health care policy*, London: King's Fund Institute

Laing and Buisson (1995), *Laing's Review of Private Healthcare 1995*, London: Laing and Buisson

Landt, J, Percival, R, Schofield, D and Wilson, D (1995), *Income Inequality in Australia: The Impact of Non-Cash Subsidies for Health and Housing*, NATSEM Discussion Paper No.5, Canberra: University of Canberra

Le Grand, J (1982), *The Strategy of Equality: Redistribution and the social services*, London: Allen and Unwin

Netten, A (1995), *Unit Costs of Community Care 1995*, Canterbury: University of Kent, PSSRU

O'Donnell, O and Propper, C (1991), 'Equity and the distribution of UK National Health Service resources', *Journal of Health Economics*, Vol. 10

Office of Health Economics (1996), *Compendium of Health Statistics*, London: Office of Health Economics

Office of Population Censuses and Surveys [OPCS] (1991), *1991 Census: Communal Establishments in Great Britain, Volume 1 of 2*, London: HMSO

Neil, J, Sinclair, I, Gorbach, P and Williams, J (1988), *A Need for Care? Elderly Applicants for Local Authority Homes*, Aldershot: Avebury

NHS Executive (1994), *HCHS Revenue Resource Allocation: Weighted Capitation Formula*, Leeds: NHS Executive

Peacock, S and Smith, P (1995), *The Resource Allocation Consequences of the New NHS Needs Formula*, York: University of York, Centre for Health Economics

Powell, M (1995), 'The strategy of equality revisited', *Journal of Social Policy*, vol.24, part 2, pp.163-185

Propper, C and Upward, R (1993), '*Modelling Health and Health Care Over the Lifetime*', STICERD Welfare State Programme Research Note, WSP/RN/27, London: London School of Economics

Pryke, R (1995), *Taking the Measure of Poverty, A Critique of Low-Income Statistics: Alternative Estimates and Policy Implications*, Institute of Economic Affairs Research Monograph 51, London: Institute of Economics Affairs

Radical Statistics Health Group (1987), *Facing the Figures: What is really happening to the National Health Service?*, London: Radical Statistics

Scottish Office (1996), *Scottish Abstract of Statistics*, No.25, 1995 Edition, Edinburgh: Scottish Office

Sinclair, I et al. (1990), *The Kaleidoscope of care: a review of research on welfare provision for elderly people*, London: HMSO

Smeeding, T, et al. (1993), 'Poverty, Inequality, and Family Living Standards Impacts Across Seven Nations: The Effect of Non-Cash Subsidies for Health, Education, and Housing', *Review of Income and Wealth*, Series 39, No.3

Universities and Colleges Admissions Service [UCAS] (1994), *Statistical Supplement to the PCAS Annual Report 1992-1993*, Bristol: Polytechnics and Colleges Funding Council

UCCA (1992), *Statistical Supplement to the Thirtieth Report 1991-2*, London: UCCA

Welsh Office (1994), *Health and Personal Social Services Statistics for Wales, No.21 1994*, Cardiff: HMSO